# COMPANY-WIDE PLANNING

## PLANNING

*Concept and Process*

# Donald B. Cotton

# COMPANY-WIDE PLANNING
## Concept and Process

THE MACMILLAN COMPANY

Collier-Macmillan, Limited · *London*

THE MACMILLAN COMPANY
866 Third Avenue, New York, New York 10022

Library of Congress Catalog Card Number: 73-116782

*First Printing*

THIS BOOK IS DEDICATED TO THE MEMORY
OF MY FATHER, WHO USED TO SAY

"THE HARDER I WORK, THE
'LUCKIER' I BECOME"

# ACKNOWLEDGMENTS

The description of purpose, scope, and limitations, often found in the preface of a book such as this, is instead given §1.1. Because of the forceful impact of those specifications in shaping the entirety of this text, they were included as initial commentary of the main body.

On this page, I wish to cite those individuals and organizations that have exerted strong influence, either directly or indirectly, in the development of notions eventually incorporated in this book, and upon the book itself. The order is chronological.

Rear Admiral T. D. Davies USN, as my Commanding Officer at the Naval Aircraft Factory, who facilitated creativity and approved latitude for experience and experiment in management.

Professor A. H. Rubenstein, my initial mentor when a graduate student at MIT, greatly influenced my approach to knowledge in general and management research in particular.

Professor E. E. Hagen, my subsequent advisor at MIT, broadened perspectives in the socioeconomics of poor countries and the means of expediting development in such regions.

J. P. Austin, President of The Coca-Cola Company, and R. S. Jones, Executive Vice President of The Coca-Cola Export Company, both of whom sponsored and guided my worldwide study of business organization and management in their firm.

R. O. Barber, President of Univis, Inc., who, with unusual professionalism and patience, provided excellent facilities and unusual support for the design and installation of a relatively full-scope company-wide planning system.

S. F. Silloway, President of Investors Diversified Services, Inc., provided the entree to establish a Corporate Planning Department in his institution, and the subsequent challenge which became the opportunity bearing this book.

Gustave Simons, my attorney, encouraged and expedited the idea for and funding of this book, and its publication.


The conceptual framework evolved for the Coca-Cola study was further developed by me at Univis, with subsequent procedurization under my direction by skillful Analyst J. D. Raney. Much of this material is utilized in the first half of this book, for which I thank the organizations and individuals involved.

My outlook on social and economic function and form is deeply influenced by Max Weber, the German sociologist, and his intellectual successors. The writings of H. A. Simon are reflected in §4.1. The statistics of §16.1 are based upon a study by The New York Stock Exchange. §16.2 leans upon the thoughts of R. H. Jenrette, of Donaldson, Lufkin and Jenrette, Inc.

The manuscript was critiqued for substance and expression by: Miss M. A. Adams, Corporate Secretary, DB Cotton & Associates, Inc.; J. Paul Austin, President, The Coca-Cola Company; R. O. Barber, President, Univis, Inc.; Professor D. L. Birch, The Harvard Graduate School of Business; J. M. Birmingham, Jr., C.F.A., Executive Vice President, Institutional Networks Company; W. R. Brazzil, Vice President, Wometco Enterprises, Inc.; D. R. Bryant, Vice President-Investments, DB Cotton & Associates, Inc; N. J. Burmeister, Vice President-Administration, DB Cotton & Associates, Inc.; R. E. Busbey, C.F.A., Vice President, Broward National Bank; H. C. Cauvet, retired financial executive, formerly with General Foods Corporation, and recent Executive Secretary of The Institute of Management Sciences; Ignazio Graul, Vice President, The Coca-Cola Export Corporation; Dr. O. Hake, Technical Planning, Allgemeine Deutsche Philips Industrie GMBH; Dr. C. J. Morales, Technical Manager, Inter-American Development Bank; Professor M. Shubik, Department of Administrative Sciences, Yale University; and R. J. Vogt, Senior Vice President, Southeast Bancorporation, Inc. Their efforts, useful and important, are very appreciated.

Of course, my very cooperative, competent, and tenacious typist, Mrs. J. T. Armbruster, also deserves due recognition for completing the manuscript, as does Miss M. A. Adams for her preliminary chartwork. Miss E. F. Dreyer has my thanks for secretarial excellence in readying the manuscript for publication.

I am also obliged to cite my friends J. R. Dickson, Bobbi McQuaid, and the late E. L. Rodriguez for their sustained encouragement during this endeavor.

While all the foregoing individuals and organizations contributed to this book, they do not necessarily endorse its contents. Furthermore, their activities and organizations are not necessarily similar to those described.

*D. B. COTTON*

*ATLANTIC TOWERS*
*FORT LAUDERDALE, FLORIDA*

# CONTENTS

## ILLUSTRATIONS

# Part One

# FUNCTION AND FORM

# CHAPTER 1

# *Background*

> *To suggest that a set of principles may exist or may be discovered, which will be applicable to the task of management, particularly in a business, is to bring forth immediately the fallacious distinction often drawn between theory and practice. There are many managers who hold to the familiar cliche that a matter may be 'all right in theory but wrong in practice.' This cannot be true. If a theory is comprised of principles which explain relationships and facts and if principles are fundamental truths explaining certain phenomena, as indeed they are, there can be no inconsistency between theory and practice. The theory may be inaccurate, or it may not be applicable to a given situation, but it can hardly be right and applicable and yet impracticable.*
>
> —H. Koontz and C. O'Donnell
> *Principles of Management*

## §1.1  PURPOSE, SCOPE, AND LIMITATIONS

This book is concerned with several related areas in the field of *planning*, which is defined as a *prescriptive process intended to guide discretionary decisionmaking in deployment and management of resources.*

The purpose of this book is to develop a system concept for a formal, company-wide, comprehensive business planning function—i.e., *company-wide planning.*

Within the internal structure of the company-wide planning function, there are three major classes of organization units: (1) the Corporate level unit specifically assigned this role full time, (2) Division level units performing a planning function, full time or part time, and (3) the various staff and service units providing support for company-wide planning as a normal consequence in their prescribed activities. The corporate echelon of the company-wide planning function will be called the *Corporate Planning Department.*

The discussion will concentrate on top management considerations, and will give passing attention to Division planning and to relations between the Corporate Planning Department and staff and service units.

Within the framework of its subject focus and scope, this book has been designed

- to offer an integrated philosophy and mode of operations in business planning.
- to present a conceptual framework for description, analysis, and control of business organizations as mechanisms for deployment and management of resources.
- to define company-wide planning as a functional area of management.
- to describe organization roles and relationships for implementation of company-wide planning.

The text emphasizes substance rather than procedure, and it should particularly facilitate both the initial efforts to organize a company-wide planning system and the production of the first plan resulting from that newly installed system.

This text offers organized reflections from the author's eclectic combination of academic backgrounds, business research, and personal experience in the rapidly developing field of formal, company-wide, comprehensive business planning, rather than an overview of planning in its many forms, or an optimal approach to planning in general. Recognized as such, it is hoped this book will aid those interested in becoming acquainted with, contributing to, and applying the philosophies, concepts, techniques, and operations of business planning.

## §1.2  EVOLUTION OF BUSINESS PLANNING

Within the context of a civilization's cultural values, manifested by its social institutions, and determined through the power structure and its exercise, the role of business assumes function and form.

Economic activity is a primary means by which society adapts to change. Such activity is essentially oriented toward the future, along a continuum of time from the immediate to infinity. The dimensions, character, and sophistication of business planning within this context is dependent upon the development stage of a society, its economic sector, the relevant industry, and its particular enterprise.

From an evolutionary viewpoint, the business planning function normally passes from the entrepreneur to an ever-widening family group and on to a still broader management council in which outsiders, representing power interests or possessing desired capabilities, participate with growing influence.

In parallel, division of decision-making proceeds sufficiently to require and facilitate refinements in planning—first through repeated application within single management functions, next through involvement on a procedural basis with multifunction scope, and ultimately extending to substantive matters in an integrated company-wide manner. With each escalation in this developmental process, the formality of the system and its extent of documentation increase. While each business organization exhibits its own pattern, dwelling on some stages and apparently skipping others (and perhaps never completing maturation) this evolutionary sequence is sufficiently typical to be a general guide.

Associated with this general pattern of evolution in business planning are three crucial characteristics that tend to greater rationality, system, and consistency:

- the sharpening of objectives and orientation toward achieving them
- enlargement of the planning concept in scope and system
- delineation of planning as a separate functional area of management

## §1.3  THE COMPANY-WIDE PLANNING MOVEMENT

Firms that have gravitated toward company-wide planning have been principally those relying upon massive capital and intensive production techniques and those requiring expensive research and development of products and processes. This trend was apparently due to the sheer magnitude of necessary resources and the tremendous implications of such program commitments. Today, more and more companies face similar determinations. The accelerating rate of change in the business environment, and the new emphasis on growth and diversification, coupled with mounting sophistication in management technology, have enlarged decision-making requirements for every firm. International interests compound the complexity through addition of variables and alternatives.

Governments worldwide, both national and local, have intensified applications of formal planning. This has resulted in an environment in which planning by the private enterprise sector is encouraged and rewarded. Compatibility with government data forms and management systems is requisite, in varying degrees, for those firms desiring effective participation in the rapidly expanding interplay between business and government.

In the United States today, over two-thirds of the five hundred largest industrial companies report having company-wide planning systems, while most of the remainder indicate that they intend to do so. Moreover, many of the smaller companies, especially those characterized by rapid growth and complex technology, have established such a function. For companies of all sizes, management consulting firms have assumed a portion, and in some instances the whole, of the company-wide planning task, either through single fundamental studies or via various levels of recurrent contribution and surveillance.

## §1.4  CONTEMPORARY COMPANY-WIDE PLANNING

In its pure form, as conceived in this book, the company-wide planning function reports in a staff relationship to the chief executive, furnishing expertise, coordination, and integration for the design of company-wide attainment in all functions, echelons, and locales encompassed by the organization.

This is accomplished both through operations of the company-wide planning system and through programs for developing that system and its satellites. The former is recurrent and the latter is nonrecurrent. These operations and programs are implemented through application of management science, execution of management research, and performance of management consulting.

To be most effective, such endeavors are characterized by a total environments perspective requiring identification, description, and manipulation of substantive behavioral, technological, and financial parameters.

The de facto form of company-wide planning, however, depends upon the degree of management sophistication, the circumstances of the business environment, the developmental stage of the host organization, the customary division of labor within it, and the availability of qualified personnel. The function's task emphasis and its location within the organization structure are reflections of these factors.

For example, many Corporate Planning Departments are occupied principally with acquisition and merger projects, others perform management consulting only, some are almost wholly engaged in long-run market research, while a few execute systems analyses and perform short-run operations scheduling.

Location in the organization structure, and communication linkages between units, are inextricably tied to task emphasis. As a result, reporting arrangements for the Corporate Planning Department can range from service as an appendage of the topmost governing body to subfunctional status within a subordinate division.

Because of the impact potential of full scope company-wide planning, the effectiveness of that function can only be a direct reflection of top management comprehension and support.

## §1.5 BENEFITS GAINED FROM COMPANY-WIDE PLANNING

Company-wide planning will result in a mix of costs and benefits determined by the environmental circumstances, skill in application, and standards for evaluation. The real costs of company-wide planning transcend those disclosed through conventional accounting. Among the most directly expensive are executive time devoted to planning-related matters, and support from staff and service units.

Change is painful. Because it is the focal point of change, the price of company-wide planning includes dissonance and strain throughout the organization. However, cost—tangible and intangible, explicit and implicit—must be judged relative to benefits derived in order to be fairly appraised.

The benefits of company-wide planning reflect values from the philosophy of science, modern management theory, and normal business practice. In an effective system

- Detection of problems, major and minor, is made more probable sufficiently in advance to spur timely remedy.
- Rationality, system, and consistency are promoted and facilitated.
- Recall of values, facts, and reasoning is enabled through documentation.

- Political controversy may be mitigated through the resulting depersonalization and group pressure.
- Leadership may be augmented by system-precipitated requirements for decisions.
- Management development is enhanced for those associated with this multifaceted activity.
- Greater compatibility of management systems and data forms with those of other businesses and government is made more likely.
- Financial community relations are aided through the broader scope, data compatibility, and confidence engendered.

In summary, company-wide planning is likely to make more effective the process of resource deployment and the management of those resources once deployed.

# CHAPTER 2

# *Basic Precepts*

> The ideas of economists and political philosophers, both when they are right and when they are wrong, are more powerful than is commonly understood. Indeed the world is ruled by little else. Practical men, who believe themselves to be quite exempt from any intellectual influences are usually the slaves of some defunct economist. Madmen in authority, who hear voices in the air, are distilling their frenzy from some academic scribbler of a few years back. I am sure that the power of vested interests is vastly exaggerated compared with the gradual encroachment of ideas.
>
> — John Maynard Keynes, *General Theory of Employment, Interest, and Money*

## §2.1 COMPANY-WIDE PLANNING DEFINED

Our definition of company-wide planning, stated earlier, rests upon three key elements: company-wide planning is a *prescriptive process* intended to guide *discretionary decision-making* in deployment and management of *resources.*

The concept that company-wide planning is a *prescriptive process* is a fundamental one since successful planning requires

- specification of future activity with sufficient lead time and precision to be technologically feasible, administratively possible, and objectively beneficial, and
- continuous development, monitoring, and adjustment of objectives, plans, and implementations which facilitate achievement on a sustained basis

Because company-wide planning is intended to guide *discretionary decision-making* it is assumed that (1) decision-making is desirable, and (2) the boundaries of discretion are specified for each relevant managerial role. While both these premises are vital to the system concept developed in this book, neither need occur under other circumstances, and in fact are questionable in many environments.

Latitude of discretion can generally increase with the time horizon, because of the possible weakening of behavioral, technological, and financial constraints resulting from many factors such as negotiation, reorganization, and research.

The term *resource* alludes to any means through which benefit is derived. In this sense, every factor—actual or potential, tangible or intangible—can be a resource.

The deployment of resources, as guided by company-wide planning, presumes that resources are both (1) identifiable, and (2) allocable.

Identification of resources is relative to organization objectives, processes available for resource transformation, and managerial competence. Thus, the quality and extent of resources can be meaningfully assayed only in view of the ends sought, manner of utilization, and character of skills available.

Resources, even if *identifiable*, may not be administratively *allocable* within the range which is technologically feasible and economically beneficial. Such restraints, if sufficiently pervasive, will significantly limit the scope of planning and delineation of resources.


## §2.2   SPHERE OF COMPANY-WIDE PLANNING

The sphere of company-wide planning encompasses *all significant influences*, external and internal, effecting sustained surveillance for rationality, system, and consistency, of

- objectives
- missions
- policies
- strategies
- estimates

The scope thus includes behavioral, technological, and financial parameters that meaningfully characterize the environment outside and within the organization. This approach necessitates matching controls for detecting anomalies in rationality, system, and consistency, within and between organization units and time periods.

Company-wide planning, then, extends far beyond that usually afforded by conventional accounting, both in breadth and time horizon. While controls emanating from traditional accounting are indispensable in appropriate applications, for company-wide planning these internally oriented methods must be augmented by (1) "sensing" mechanisms for comprehending the external environment, and (2) internal means for control of corporate image and operating concept.

## §2.3   BEYOND THE SPHERE

The concept of company-wide planning developed in this book *excludes* from this function

- authority for the substance of *value* premises
- unrelated and nonrecurring *projects*
- the implementation of procedural *routine*

The planning function should not be viewed as responsible for determining the substance of fundamental value premises. As defined in §4.1, such premises voice preferences rather than empirical considerations. Rather, company-wide planning, through its analytical approach,

- detects conflicts, omissions, gaps, and overlaps in the organization's value premises, stated and implied
- resolves these discrepancies, in conjunction with top management and other appropriate sources, and
- phrases these fundamental preferences in a formal and precise manner, with regard for consistency and priority ordering

Thus, the company-wide planning function expresses, but does not originate, the basic values of the organization. Therefore, responsibility for the substance of value premises is beyond its sphere. Detection, reduction, and employment of value premises is discussed in Chapter 11.

Company-wide planning has been defined as a prescriptive process, which requires continuous development, monitoring, and adjustment of objectives, plans, and implementations. In these terms, it was noted that the function is accomplished through

- recurrent operations of the company-wide planning system, and
- nonrecurrent projects in developing that system and its satellites

Few acts of top management can be more detrimental to the establishment of systematic comprehensive planning than dominating the function with nonrecurrent projects. This typically results in disruption of output continuity, fragmentation of subject scope, and incomparability of time horizons. The "coup de grace" to company-wide planning can occur when assignments of nonrecurrent projects unrelated to planning are foisted upon the function. This trades technical expertise and function discipline for the diffuse and polyglot "special study" expedient, which is beyond the sphere of systematic company-wide planning per se.

Once evolved, proven, and perhaps institutionalized by the company-wide planning function, procedural routine should be placed and implemented elsewhere in the organization, to the extent circumstances permit. This policy will assist in the preservation of the conceptual orientation, technical expertise, and function discipline which are desirable in company-wide planning.

In particular, while the sphere of company-wide planning extends far beyond that provided by conventional accounting, the latter is not encompassed by planning. On the contrary, within context of the planning function, controllership is a closely associated but distinctly separate support to which many of the procedural elements in planning are transferred for application throughout the organization.

## §2.4   THE PRICE OF CHANGE

Because company-wide planning guides discretionary decision-making, the function is the focal point of change. While much has been and will be said about its causes, impacts, ramifications, and side effects, on balance *change is painful* to the great majority of those immediately and directly involved. Thus, if comprehensive planning is conceptually oriented, technically expert, and functionally disciplined, it cannot help but be surrounded with dissonance and strain.

The rate of change can be increased by a combination of top management determination and tenacity, by suitable communication of intentions throughout the organization, and by appropriate personnel development, reward, and punishment. Change has a price, and it tends to seem especially high to those directly involved with the company-wide planning function.

# CHAPTER 3

# Organization for Planning

*It should be observed that these different orders are by no means to be understood precisely as the geometrical figures indicate them. A general who would expect to arrange his line of battle as regularly as upon paper or on a drill-ground would be greatly mistaken, and would be likely to suffer defeat. . . . and when such figures are used in discussing the combinations of tactics it can only be for the purpose of giving definite expression to an idea by the use of a known symbol . . . if it seems absurd to desire to mark out upon the ground orders of battle in such regular lines as would be used in tracing them on a sketch, a skillful general may nevertheless bear in mind the orders which have been indicated above and may so combine his troops on the battlefield that the arrangement shall be similar to one of them.*

—A. H. Jomini, *The Art of War*

## §3.1 A SIMPLIFIED SYSTEM CONCEPT

The essential purpose of company-wide planning is to increase the probability that organization objectives will be attained. Toward this end, plans for future resource deployment are *continuously* developed and appraised for their compatibility with organization objectives and constraints.

The development of objectives, selection of parameters, and establishment of performance standards are discussed in subsequent chapters. For the overview of a company-wide planning system presented in this chapter, it is assumed that these already exist, even if crude, and that their nature is consistent with normal business practice. Given these conditions, the company-wide planning system

1. requires *estimates* of future organization performance and resources, over relevant time periods,
2. *matches* these estimates with organization objectives during relevant time periods, and thereby
3. determines the *gap* between these objectives and estimates, as to both magnitude and timing, which then
4. *precipitates* means for closing this gap, by redeployment of organization resources and/or adjustment of performance standards, modification of parameters, or change in objectives and constraints.

The company-wide planning system and its satellites are designed and operated for the express purpose of accomplishing these tasks. The process is depicted graphically in Figure 3.A. While conceptually sequential, these steps can, to some extent, overlap in parallel.

It has been emphasized that company-wide planning is a prescriptive process, and that use of the system should be continuous. Each concerted flow through the system is demarked as a *cycle*, its tangible end product being a

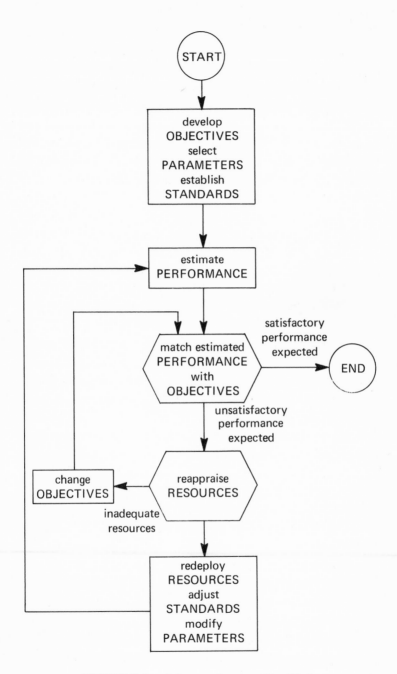

**FIGURE 3.A. A System Concept Simplifed.**

company-wide plan. Subsequent changes result from *recycling* the previous effort, in whole or in part, to produce a successor plan. If the desired magnitude, complexity, and frequency of recycling become too onerous, or if a shorter reaction time is sought, the planning system must itself be significantly altered or redesigned—administratively and technologically.

## §3.2   A SYSTEM CONCEPT EXPANDED

The simplified system concept described in the preceding section provides only a structural overview of the planning process. It must be further developed within the organization for truly effective application.

Estimates of expected performance are clearly necessary for implementation of the company-wide planning function. It is useful to segment estimates of future performance and resources into three categories:

**passive expectations**   These are estimates of performance and resources associated with *current and incipient* processes, products, markets, and locales.

**expansion expectations**   These are estimates of performance and resources associated with *related* but not incipient processes, products, markets, and locales.

**diversification expectations**   These are estimates of performance and resources associated with processes, products, markets, and locales *unrelated* with current and incipient activities.

Differentiation in accord with these classes is often difficult and sometimes arbitrary—even when definitions are precise and oriented toward specific organizations.

The planning cycle can commence with description of prospects for the relevant base industry(ies) in which the organization participates. Utilizing this material, passive expectations for the organization are derived. Through comparison with objectives, a gap between objectives and expectations is determined as to both magnitude and timing. Thereafter, expectations for further expansion in the base industry are added to the passive expectations to obtain total expectations for the organization in the base industry. Again, objectives and expectations are matched to determine a gap between them. The gap may then be filled by diversification into areas unrelated with the organization's current or incipient activities.

During the planning process, resource identification and allocation are simulated with respect to each category of performance expectations—the passive, expansion, and diversification alternatives. Here, as Figure 3.B indicates, resource identification and allocation are constrained by three primary factors:

1. *mission* of the organization
2. management *policies*
3. *standards* for performance

Overall strategy for the organization is reflected in the choice and mix of passive, expansion, and diversification activities. The planning process itself is channeled by specification of missions, formulation of policies, and criteria for performance. The organization's thrust is focused through development of objectives, selection of parameters, and establishment of performance standards.

In this system, all is oriented toward the determination and elimination of the gap between objectives and

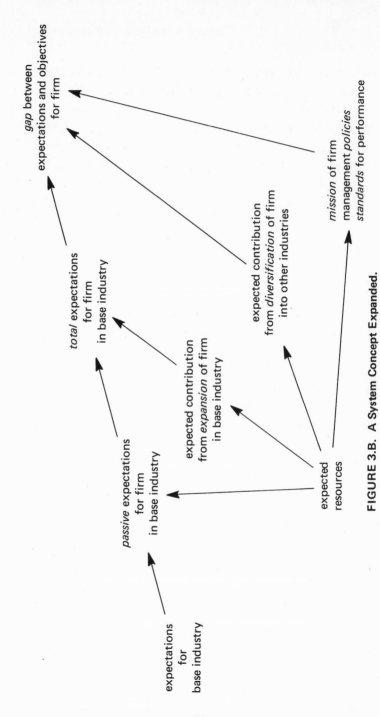

FIGURE 3.B. A System Concept Expanded.

estimates, as to both magnitude and timing. The magnitude of the gap is multidimensional. It is measured through each of the parameters selected by topmost management and institutionalized by the company-wide planning system. The nature of this gap—qualitative and quantitative—will be expressed in terms of the parameters by which it is measured, including the relevant time period.

The multidimensional character of this gap will probably result in remedies which include incomparabilities, interdependencies, and circularities. Expertise in implementing the process of planning should reduce these conditions to their fundamental issues, and precipitate them for top management consideration.

This expanded system concept is in essence the same as that simple overview described in the preceding section. Both systems operate, recycle, and ultimately indicate their own obsolescence, in like fashion.

## §3.3 THE CHARACTER AND COMPOSITION OF INTEGRATED PLANNING

The company-wide planning process is an all-encompassing integrated endeavor, supported by interlocking subordinate activities aligned by

- technological process
- product identity
- market character
- geographic locale

The delineation of activities in these terms may be superficially submerged within larger groupings of apparent company organization. Regardless of visibility, their fundamental nature requires specific treatment in the company-wide planning process. The classical management functions can be viewed as subforms of technological process, and in this sense can be added to the above list if this assists in the process of planning.

All of these foci operate simultaneously, contributing to the company-wide planning process, even if implicitly. Each focus must be accounted for. The extent of formal delineation, and the explicit treatment given any one, depends upon its relative priority under the company's current organization strategy.

Each subordinate activity is characterized by its own dimensions—its scope, depth, and time horizon. The comparable dimensions for each of these subordinate activities need not coincide, and most often do not. For example, in a given organization, marketing may be broadest, manufacturing most refined, and research more visionary.

No matter what future span is chosen for a particular activity, the degree of detail ordinarily fades as the time horizon increases. The reliability of inputs and estimates decreases as considerations are projected further. So does ability to implement on schedule the actions ultimately prescribed. For example, in a ten-year plan, the first year may be segmented into quarterly intervals, the second two years in semi-annual increments, the fourth and fifth years as annual, the sixth and seventh consolidated together, as are the eighth, ninth, and tenth years.

The prime plan, that which exists at the corporate level, may extend farthest into the future. The time horizon of each subordinate plan is terminated at the point in time where reliabilities of inputs, estimates, or schedules fall below limits acceptable to the superordinate organization. For example, in a given organization, the corporate plan may reach out ten years, while for the Western European Area the span could be seven years, and, in contrast, planning for the Brazil Region may cover only three years.

The idea of reliability in this book is analogous with risk, i.e., predictability, discussed in Chapter 6. The arguments, pro and con, for this trade of equal reliability for unequal time horizons, sacrificing administrative uniformity for technical veracity, are examined in § 7.5.

In summary, the concept of *integrated planning* rests upon two precepts:

1. interlocking subordinate activities aligned in accord with the priorities of organization strategy
2. time horizons determined by the limits of acceptable reliability

Thus, through this system, long- and short-range, strategy and operations, are melded into an integrated and recurrently updated whole.

## § 3.4 STRUCTURAL POSITION OF THE CHIEF PLANNER

The interaction of the de facto chief planner with the de facto chief executive—no matter what their nominal titles—is a critically important and integral aspect of the planning system. In general, it is strongly advised that the chief planner report in a *direct staff relationship to the chief executive*, as shown in Figure 3.C. Of the many reasons for this structural configuration, five major arguments are:

1. To establish and sustain *credibility* for his function, the chief planner's structural location in the organization should closely coincide with that of the chief executive's in order to afford a similar perception of activities, internal and external.
2. The direct reporting relation facilitates development and maintenance of the *rapport* so necessary for effective interaction between the chief executive and his planner.
3. As the planning function is a prime focal point of substantive and procedural change, a direct relation with the chief executive bestows upon the chief planner an advantageous *stature* enabling him to deal with probable resistance which could otherwise stymie progress.
4. This siting of the chief planner, untied to other organization units, evokes a *neutral image* unique in dispelling rivalry and gaining cooperation.
5. From the instant of inception, this organization format deeply commits the chief executive to a definitive, vigorous, and highly visible *endorsement* of company-wide planning as a management function, and to the chief planner as an individual.

There are circumstances, however, where this strong recommendation for direct reporting relation with the chief executive could be disregarded in favor of other organization configurations:

1. Where the chief executive lacks the professional interest, management competence, or political effectiveness to supervise and support the planning function, the chief planner is better off elsewhere.
2. If the chief executive is physically unable, because

of health or age, to continuously spur the dynamism company-wide planning implies, he and the function will be incompatible.

3. When destructive personality clashes are apt to develop between the chief executive and his planner, some other organizational arrangement is advisable.

4. If an individual in a central but lesser role be groomed for imminent promotion to chief executive, his supervision of the planning function could be excellent for all concerned.

5. And finally, if company-wide planning has been so thoroughly institutionalized that it has been accepted as routine by the organization, it could perhaps be treated as just another staff function and report to a lower echelon.

Thus far, and throughout the remainder of this book, the top role in the company-wide planning function is referred to as *chief planner*.

This neutral appellation affords accurate functional description without implying hierarchical position and legal status. Whether the chief planner should be an officer, and/or titled Vice President, depends upon company circumstances. In general, for a virile and comprehensive company-wide planning function, officer designation and Vice President title provide highly desirable status for internal management application, and in representing the organization externally.

## §3.5   FORMAL ROLE OF THE CHIEF PLANNER

The following description of the chief planner's role

coincides with that for the entire company-wide planning function, as we have defined it. Depending upon the quantity and emphasis of workload, various organization configurations can be developed to support this type of planning effort, some of which are discussed in § 3.6.

This full-scope description is based upon assumptions that the host organization takes company-wide planning seriously, and that competent and aggressive leadership will enable the function to be truly implemented in this comprehensive form. Conversely, the suggested role specifications must be altered to accommodate (1) skepticism in the organization, (2) absence of comprehending and effective support from the chief executive, and (3) pre-existing management functions which relate to and compete with company-wide planning.

As the organization's top technical expert and advisor in his field, the core responsibilities of the chief planner are to conceptualize, structure, and procedurize substance and system for planning and planning-related matters throughout the company. Effectively implemented, these activities facilitate planning throughout the organization in a rational, systematic, and consistent manner.

Basic values are the foundation of substance in decision-making. Substance should initially be provided through the efforts of responsible operating personnel, with technical and administrative staff support. The detection, reduction, and inclusion of the organization's basic values is discussed in Chapter 11. However, through lack of professional interest, managerial competence, or political effectiveness, those executives may avoid such fundamental issues, thus relegating these to the planning function. If this occurs, the planning function then more closely approaches the de facto origin of leadership in the organization.

As a source of technical expertise, the planning function may occasionally, on a *nonrecurrent* basis, execute assignments from the chief executive regarding

- formulation of objectives, missions, policies, strategies, estimates, and controls
- impact simulation of major alternatives
- macro and micro economic analyses
- strategy for organization structures
- appraisal and procedurization of decision-making processes

All of these are "project" assignments which may be undertaken in collaboration with operating personnel, relevant staff, and external consultants. The planning function could receive these assignments because of technical expertise, or simply because of available manpower. Also, some such assignments may be given to the planning function because it is more neutral than the competing interest groups to whom particularly controversial assignments would otherwise be delegated.

Assuming a combination of the necessary technical expertise in the planning function, and its simultaneous unavailability elsewhere in the organization, the chief planner may offer, in a consistent and timely manner,

- surveillance of the macroeconomic environment
- inter-industry comparisons
- commentary on financial markets

The planning function maintains direct interest in these topics for their immediate application in strategy-making, in acquisition and divestment analysis, and in financial community relations.

The chief planner confers and consults on planning-related matters in all functions, echelons, and locales encompassed by the company. This interaction of the planning function and the remaining organization facilitates transfer of technical expertise, and encourages the perspective, sensitivity, and rapport so desirable for company-wide planning.

At the same time, the chief planner confers and *consults* on planning-related matters with customers and suppliers, when directed by the chief executive. In general, the advantages which accrue to this external activity are similar to those of the internal consulting described above. In specific instances, a major problem between the company and given customer or supplier may be planning-related either at the interface or internally. Under assignment, the planning function may study resolution of the difficulty, perhaps jointly with operating personnel and the outside organization involved.

Given establishment of a system concept for company-wide planning and institutionalization of supporting procedures, the chief planner recurrently

- provides techniques for development of contributions to company-wide planning
- phrases, with approval of the chief executive, company-wide assumptions and constraints governing each planning cycle
- maintains liaison with each Division, through those specifically responsible for the Division Planning Function
- schedules and coordinates corporate level and inter-division contributions to company-wide planning.
- advises the chief executive concerning the substance,

format, and quality of all contributions to company-wide planning

This last sub-task can often be a source of great friction between the planning function and, the rest of the organization. The chief planner—as top technical expert and advisor in his field—establishes, through the chief executive, specifications for subject matter, data array, reliability of estimates, and schedules for contributions to company-wide planning. Clearly, his recommendations in these respects should consider the composite of surrounding circumstances and opinions.

Responsible operating personnel—supported by relevant staff—are, of course, expected to input the company-wide planning system as approved by the chief executive. Even with skill in human relations, considerable organization discipline is still necessary to enforce compliance. This is especially crucial in the exercise of quality control and schedule adherence by the planning function. Political crises of an extreme sort can be precipitated by planners' surveillance of intangibles related to rationality and reliability.

The chief planner participates in relations with the *financial community* in general, and in collaboration with other responsible personnel he

- develops, interprets, and communicates with the financial community *analyses* relevant to the company
- performs *liaison* with relevant personnel within and external to the company, where comprehensive knowledge of these areas is desirable

Financial community relations, and the role of the

planning function therein, is the subject of Chapter 16. Here we note briefly that the chief planner complements rather than supplants the Controller, Treasurer, Financial Vice President, and Director of Public Relations in their respective contributions to financial community relations.

## § 3.6  INTERNAL STRUCTURE OF COMPANY-WIDE PLANNING

The company-wide planning function, described in § 3.5, coincides with role of the chief planner. Internal structure within the company-wide planning function depends upon the quantity of workload and the emphasis of direction. These, in turn, are determined by hospitality of the host organization, degree of comprehension and effective support from the chief executive, and extent of pre-existing management functions which relate and compete with company-wide planning. In life cycle terms, referred to more fully in Chapter 5, the internal structure of company-wide planning will manifest the evolutionary stage of the function itself.

Within the internal structure of the company-wide planning function, there are three classes of organization units: (1) the Corporate level unit specifically assigned this role full time; (2) Division level units performing the planning function, full time or part time; and (3) the various staff and service units providing support for the planning function as a normal consequence in their prescribed activities. The *Corporate level echelon* of the company-wide planning function is called the *Corporate Planning Department.*

The Division Planning Function is an inseparable component of the Division Chief's role, operating under the technical surveillance of the Corporate Planning

Department. As such, the Division Chief has discretion to accommodate the planning function by recourse to his own efforts, by multiple assignments of personnel from within his organization unit, and by aid from the Corporate Planning Department. However implemented, the Division is responsible for furnishing contributions to the company-wide planning function as approved by the chief executive.

Staff and service group relationships to the Corporate and Division planning functions are covered peripherally with remarks at the end of this chapter regarding the administrative subfunction within the Corporate Planning Department.

The origin and evolution of business planning was sketched in Chapter 1. For illustration, three possible stages of increasing maturity are presented, each with a commensurately developed internal organization structure. But all of the role descriptions and structural formats presented in this section are intended as illustrative— indicative and suggestive—rather than definitive in any absolute sense. The following assumes the chief executive's commitment to a formal, company-wide, and comprehen- sive planning function.

A *first stage* Corporate Planning Department is represented in Figure 3.3.C, where one individual—the chief planner—is responsible for execution of the entire company-wide planning role described in §3.5. Here, the planning function is not characterized by any structured relation with other units, and has yet to establish an image. Such lack of clear identity, at this point, actually facilitates effective orientation between the planner and host organization, especially with the chief executive. (Activities during this period are the subject of Chapters 10 and 11.)

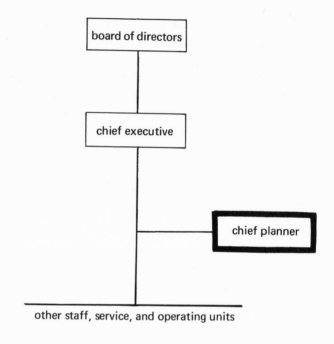

**FIGURE 3.C. Corporate Planning Department, Internal Structure, Illustrative Stage 1.**

To preserve this bland posture while still appraising circumstances, the chief planner may wish to draw administrative and clerical support from pools available elsewhere in the organization. Especially where technical proficiency or security of information are considerations, external sources may be utilized.

The second individual likely to be employed in the Corporate Planning Department would be a *Research Assistant*, with responsibilities as follows:

■ coordinates administrative support within the Corporate Planning Department

- executes closely directed economic and financial research
- plans and supervises administration and maintenance of statistical and graphical routines
- supervises and aids reproduction of literature and presentations
- performs executive secretary duties

The Research Assistant, as a Corporate Planning Department contact with middle management, supervisory personnel, and clerical elements, must be efficient in an unusually broad span of activities and echelons. Knowledge of the organization gained through prior service, while exceedingly beneficial in this role, must be weighed against the disadvantage of security leaks to former associates. The Research Assistant is immediately a key figure in company-wide planning, and remains so throughout the life of this function.

The mutual orientation characterizing first stage activities of the company-wide planning function provides a foundation for the subsequent formative period discussed in Chapter 11, and the first participation of the entire organization described in Chapter 12. During this interval, the quantity of work load accelerates, and the sphere is enlarged to encompass procedural activities emphasizing system design, data search, information processing, and management training.

It is probable that the third Corporate Planning Department member will be a *Corporate Planning Analyst (General)*, reporting to the chief planner, and assigned subordinate duties within and throughout his superior's role at a *procedural level*. He would exercise broad expertise in *management science* (with particular skills in mathematical methods) and would be required to routinize and communicate these to all parts of the organization.

Because of heightened administrative and clerical workload occasioned by development of the company-wide planning system and addition of the Corporate Planning Analyst, the next Corporate Planning Department employee to be hired could be a *Clerical Technician* reporting to and supporting the Research Assistant.

The growing company-wide planning function will generate mounting pressure for more rational, systematic, and consistent appraisals of the external environment and company's relative position therein. With this in view, it could be appropriate if the Department acquired a *Corporate Planning Analyst (Marketing)*, to concentrate upon marketing and distribution analysis through expert applications of econometrics and management science. This *second stage* Corporate Planning Department internal organization structure is depicted in Figure 3.D.

With revision, refinement, and recycling of the first company-wide efforts, may come increased comprehension of and support for the function, as well as greater proficiency in planning at the Division level. At this point, it could be propitious to reorient and enlarge the internal structure of the Corporate Planning Department better to support technically and to control functionally other organization units contributing to company-wide planning.

By this time, it is apparent that there are two distinctive types of work flowing through the Corporate Planning Department:

1. *recurrent* operations of the company-wide planning system, and
2. *nonrecurrent* projects in development of that system and its satellites

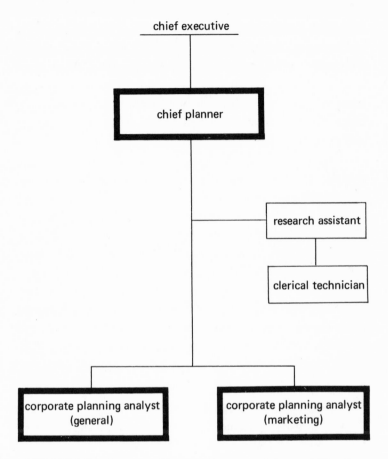

**FIGURE 3.D. Corporate Planning Department, Internal Structure, Illustrative Stage 2.**

Recurrent aspects of the company-wide planning system occur at two levels of substance, strategy and operations. These are differentiated in subsequent paragraphs of this section.

It has been pointed out that nonrecurrent projects unrelated to planning can be exceedingly damaging to, and so, should be excluded from, the sphere of company-wide planning. Even when nonrecurrent projects are planning-related, assignment of such projects to those responsible for operating and maintaining the company-wide planning system will result in disruption of output continuity, fragmentation of subject scope, and incomparability of time horizons. Organizational means must be created to accommodate this nonrecurrent unrelated work in another expeditious manner.

The organization configuration illustrative of this *third stage* is pictured in Figure 3.E.

The main subfunctions of the third stage Corporate Planning Department organization structure are now defined in context with the role description for company-wide planning of § 3.5.

The *strategic planning* subfunction broadly specifies, on a *recurrent* basis, preferred means of achieving desired objectives. This subfunction is oriented toward *deployment* of resources. Strategic planning

- derives an overview of intelligence regarding the external environment
- establishes parameters for objectives, and standard values for them
- delineates missions and related constraints
- identifies resources and their allocability
- formulates policies to achieve objectives within specified constraints

The *operations planning* subfunction narrowly specifies, on a *recurrent* basis, preferred means of implementing strategic plans. This subfunction is oriented toward *management* of resources once they have been deployed strategically. Operations planning

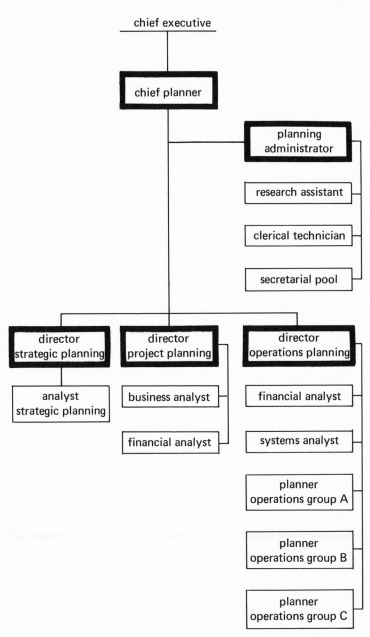

**FIGURE 3.E.  Corporate Planning Department, Internal Structure, Illustrative Stage 3**

- derives detailed intelligence regarding the immediate environment
- establishes subparameters for goals, and standard values for them
- delineates operating constraints within the context of missions
- develops systems for managing deployed resources
- formulates procedures to achieve goals within given constraints and through the foregoing systems

Operations planning, to more effectively support operations units throughout the organization, can be aligned to coincide with major groupings composing the company. For example, note the operations planners, one each for company groups A, B, and C, in Figure 3.E.

The *project planning* subfunction conducts research and analyses, on a *nonrecurrent* basis, regarding

- effects of internal environment upon feasibility of organization objectives, the process of planning for their achievement, and the most appropriate rate of change
- simulation of the probable impact of new processes, products, markets, and locales, upon organization performance
- solidifying preliminary plans and processes, products, markets, and locales, to fill the gap between opportunity, expectations, and organization objectives

Thus, project planning may include search and initiation of acquisition and divestment activities in accord with specifications from the strategic planning subfunction.

The *administrative* subfunction performs routinized administration and communication regarding planning-related matters. This unit

- coordinates, schedules, monitors, and provides liaison for all Division level contributions to company-wide planning
- coordinates, schedules, monitors, and provides liaison for all activities internal to the Corporate Planning Department
- formats, edits, unifies, and distributes reports and displays
- is secretary to all Division level committees directly concerned with the company-wide planning function

The administrative aspects of company-wide planning, both to the overall function and within the Corporate Planning Department, will likely become onerous, making highly desirable the establishment of a group expressly for this purpose. Because of the dominance of relations with middle management, supervisory personnel, and clerical elements, inadequate attention to this interface can generate friction, cause great inefficiency, and even paralyze activities on a wide scale.

It is reiterated that all of the role descriptions and structural configurations presented in this section are intended as illustrative—indicative and suggestive—rather than definitive in any absolute sense.

# Part Two

# CONCEPTUAL FRAMEWORK

# CHAPTER 4

# *Fundamental Objectives*

> The summits of various kinds of business
> are, like the tops of mountains, much more
> alike than the parts below ... the bare
> principles are much the same; it is only the
> rich variegated details of the lower strata
> that so contrast with one another. But it
> needs traveling to know that the summits are
> the same. Those who live on one mountain
> believe that their mountain is wholly unlike
> all others.
>
> —Walter Bagehot, *The English Constitution*

## §4.1 STRUCTURE AND CLASSIFICATION OF OBJECTIVES

A truly effective approach to company-wide planning requires an integrated concept of organization, and a compatible means of stratifying decisions in accord with their value content, with an analogous classification of objectives.

An organization can be viewed as a group of human beings which exhibits a special pattern of communication as well as other relationships. A particular organization is delineated from the general social system by its participants' unique pattern of *interrelations* within the organization, and their orientation toward a specific array of *objectives*. Changes in environment, interrelations, and objectives will each have an impact upon the organization, with consequences ranging in degree from mere adjustment to total destruction.

The organization utilizes its resources to achieve desired objectives. The deployment of resources and their management occur by decision. Decisions can be characterized in two major classes. Those in which preferences are formulated are concerned with *value*, while those related to empirical choices are considerations of *fact*. The former dominate in fundamentals, and the latter in implementation.

The integration of human behavior in an organization can be viewed as a process which occurs in three decisional steps:

1. *fundamental* decisions prescribe values and boundaries for subordinate acts.
2. *strategic* decisions, within context of fundamentals, broadly specify preferred means of achieving desired objectives.
3. *operations* decisions narrowly specify preferred means of implementing approved strategies.

Plans emanating from and supporting the respective levels of decisions are stratified in a parallel manner. Extending the scheme, the structure of objectives for an organization can be visualized in pyramidal form with three hierarchical layers:

1. fundamental objectives
2. strategic objectives
3. operations objectives

As defined in §12.2, an *objective* is a broad aim or ultimate end toward which a plan is designed and implemented. The remainder of this chapter deals with the institutional assumptions that underlie, the basic parameters for, and the general statement of, *fundamental objectives.*

## §4.2  INSTITUTIONAL ASSUMPTIONS

As described earlier, fundamental objectives are formulations of preferences which prescribe values and boundaries for subsidiary acts. Being pregnant with value premises, they reflect and are generated within the context of institutions characterizing the host society.

An *institution* is an established *norm of conduct* recognized by a distinguishable social group. Allowing for simplification and brevity, the behavior of large publicly owned U.S. corporations suggests derivation from three prime institutions:

- the ideology of *private enterprise*
- the economics of *capitalism*
- the administrative form of *bureaucracy*

Other influences may be dominant in specific enterprises, and even for broad groups of firms, over significant time intervals. However, it is submitted that the validity of these suppositions over the long run is sufficient to constitute this triad as the foundation of effort in large publicly owned United States corporations.

The ideological assumption of *private enterprise* pertains simultaneously to cultural, political, and economic concepts, which can be expressed in terms of

- *free choice* by the consumer in the market
- *private ownership* of the means of production, and free choice in its employment
- the return of a *"fair" profit* to those owners

The economic assumption of *capitalism* rests upon the existence of basic cultural values and a concomitant social structure which simultaneously encourage

- economically productive *work* as an end in itself
- *moderation* in consumption of the material rewards of production
- *reinvestment* in economically productive enterprise of the unconsumed material rewards

The administrative assumption is that of *bureaucracy*, one accepted expression of rationality in organization form, characterized by

- a structure composed of an integrated *hierarchy* of specialized offices, with legitimate authority vested in the office not the incumbent
- government of the organization through a system of *rules*, both rational and impersonal
- recruitment and promotion of personnel based upon managerial and technical *ability*

Allowing, once again, for the simplification and brevity of definitions in this section, it is maintained that their underlying validity in the American context makes the triad extremely useful as a standard reference within which the institutional assumptions of U.S. businesses may be described, compared, and analyzed.

## §4.3 INSTITUTIONS AND DIVERSIFICATION

A society possesses its own set of values and institutions that often give rise to "national character." Within a society, groups may be demarked by their own subcultures and associated norms of behavior. In parallel fashion, an occupational group may be characterized by a way of life in which the members pursue unique objectives, are governed by a particular code of ethics, and possess special skills.

In this sense, each industry has its own personality, which transcends company environment, regional attributes, and national boundaries. This unique character, in turn, influences the other social groups to which industry members belong, and in some cases may be sufficiently powerful to dominate their behavior. These ties of industry between otherwise diverse individuals are often deep and sometimes governing.

The social institutions of diversified organizations must encompass and accommodate the behavioral norms of sub groups of which they are composed. The formal planning process facilitates early detection and amelioration of institutional conflicts derived from such non-homogenous roots. The resulting conflict resolution mitigates what could otherwise be continuing friction and inefficiency that is sometimes not immediately apparent.

Coping with differing value systems and social institutions has long been an acknowledged problem for international organizations. This can also be the case within one country, though less apparent, where firms straddle more than one industry and operate in several locales with varying regional attributes.

### §4.4 COMMONALITY OF BUSINESSES

Business, as a social phenomenon, has a commonality which overreaches company codes, industrial norms, regional attributes, and national character. No matter where observed, businessmen pursue like objectives, possess related skills, and exalt broadly similar ethics.

Even in the face of social pressure or severe governmental restraints on very large companies, and allowing for a modicum of philanthropy, most business organizations are oriented toward profit, albeit with varying degrees of aggressiveness. This being so, the parameters for fundamental objectives may be considered common to all business organizations, although relative priorities between them and standard values for each may differ. Therefore, shedding the embroidery which often surrounds and sometimes may briefly dominate company aspirations, the core of business activity is *rational economic productivity* which requires, for survival and growth, motivation by and satisfaction of profit incentives.

### §4.5 FUNDAMENTAL OBJECTIVES AND PARAMETERS

In §4.2, it was submitted that, over the long run, the institutional triad of private enterprise, capitalism, and bureaucracy is the foundation of effort in large publicly held U.S. corporations. These institutional assumptions have their common focus in the *rational economic productivity* of capital, in which the primary parameters are

- $k$   *capital employed*, active and/or passive
- $r$   *risk* of capital employment
- $t$   *time* span for capital employment
- $y$   *yield* on capital employed

Acceptable bounds for capital employment may be specified through a formal circumscription of behavior—a mission statement— for which constraints are

- $s$   *scope* of activity
- $d$   *depth* of activity

The statement of mission, can contain behavioral, technological, and financial limits prescribing the "theater of operations." Using these parameters, a core statement of the organization's fundamental objective would be, in symbolic form,

given $k$
achieve $y$ over $t$ at $r$
within $s$ and $d$

The objective of each subordinate organization unit derived from, aligned with, and supporting the fundamental objective, would be expressed in similar manner.

# CHAPTER 5

# *A Capitalistic Viewpoint*

*If you can't stand the heat,
then get out of the kitchen.*
—Attributed to Harry S. Truman

## § 5.1 FINANCIAL MARKET EVALUATION

Awareness of function and form with respect to financial markets is essential for effective leadership of any economic organization in a modern society.

Financial markets are a means for exchange and evaluation of both capital sources and uses. Origins of capital are compared for capacity and cost. Applications are assessed for profit and risk. These appraisals span all possible sources and uses, occurring worldwide and continuously over a time horizon extending from the immediate to infinity.

Of course, financial market evaluations are not perfect, and sometimes, in fact, are far removed from rationality and realism. Sources of information, methods of analysis, means of forecasting, and market mechanisms themselves are all imperfect. Styles often hold sway and may change abruptly.

However, in the United States, the veracity, timeliness, and uniformity of information have improved vastly in recent years, and it is likely that this trend will continue. Investor interest, capacity, and sophistication are at an all-time high, generating a crushing demand which is forcing financial firms into greater effectiveness. And, the financial community itself is entering a managerial renaissance in philosophy, concept, structure, and technique. So, while the dynamic and far-reaching financial market has flaws, its mechanisms are excellent, and there is every probability that improvements will accelerate at a rapid pace.

The availability and cost of capital is determined by a market evaluation melding considerations such as the following:

- the international political and economic situation
- impact of government policies, especially monetary and fiscal
- expectations for relevant industries
- general evaluation of a specific company
- capacity of that company regarding this financing
- image of its management in the financial community

Thus, the success and underwriting costs of a new equity issue, the redistribution of an old one, or the interest rates required for debt, all reflect a composite appraisal of a company within the context of its total environment.

Likewise the current market price of a publicly owned company's securities is a continuing reflection of expected performance for the firm itself, of the vehicle in question, and of the relevant segment of that financial market versus other possible applications of investment.

Thus, it is our contention that over a reasonable period of time the financial community's evaluation of a business is the most encompassing assessment that can be made. Further, within this framework, for a large publicly owned U.S. corporation, the most comprehensive single indicator of expected business success is the ratio of common stock price to per share earnings: the *price-earnings multiple.*

## §5.2  GROWTH COMPANIES AND GROWTH STOCKS

History demonstrates that a life cycle characterizes natural and social phenomena. This much-discussed pattern can be visualized as a continuum composed of periods described by the terms basal, growth, maturity, decline, and senility. Much recent national, regional, and business planning is directed towards the modification of this sequence through attempts to

- arrest the life cycle at a favorable stage
- sustain the longevity of an attractive phase
- reverse the cycle to a more desirable position
- reactivate the cycle into its normal evolution

The life cycle notion has been applied to economies, industries, and firms. Every major industry was once in a growth stage, and some still are. Others may be at their apexes, and some are in decline or stagnant. Within industries, firms experience a similar pattern. However, while it is likely that an industry's evolution will channel the development of its member firms, the life cycle of industry and firm need not necessarily coincide, and in fact often demonstrate startling contrasts.

The phrases *growth company* and *growth stock*, in general use within business management and the financial community, while derived from the same base, diverge in meaning and implication. In practice, these phrases so lack consistency and precision that in analysis they should be specifically defined for the particular purpose at hand.

The usual measure of growth in security analysis revolves about the rate of increase in earnings per common share. The annual compounded U.S. growth rate in GNP since World War II has been around 4 percent in constant dollars or 6.5 percent in current dollars, and one standard for growth stock designation requires at least these results. On the other hand, Wall Street ordinarily considers 7 percent the minimum. Another view specifies twice the results obtained over five to ten years by the broad common stock indexes.

Even with a long run attitude, the growth stock investor faces a dilemma. He can choose younger companies characterized by noteworthy, although relatively short, expansions and thus risk deception by temporary success. Or contrarywise, selection could be made from older companies where present power may be prelude to decline.

A key to this paradox is in the real source of company growth. Should it result from an exogenous change in the environment, then this is a relatively passive phenomenon. On the other hand, if it accrues from endogenous activities that reshape the environment to advantage, this is a more aggressive form. In the usual case, both elements appear, albeit in differing proportions according to circumstance. While the more active mode can evoke greater visibility, business success continues to be associated with both types.

The longevity of expected company growth is another crucial consideration. Growth, even over extended periods, can be due to nonrecurrent factors having little or no promise of continuity. Such circumstances, when spectacular, are called *special situations* in the financial community. To qualify as a growth company, expectations for superior earnings increases must derive from circumstances which promise continuity. In this sense, a management capable of producing consistently recurrent superior increases in earnings from a continuing succession of nonrecurrent origins might qualify its firm as a growth company.

> A *growth company,* in very general terms, is one expected to maintain superior increases in earnings per share over a substantial period of time.
> A *growth stock* is a security—usually equity—of a publicly owned growth company.

The general inference is that a growth stock will continue to increase in value parallel with business success in the underlying growth company. Over the years, this implication is generally, but not necessarily, correct. Stock prices may not follow earnings trends, due to the properties of financial markets discussed in § 5.1.

## § 5.3  GROWTH COMPANIES AND THE FINANCIAL COMMUNITY

Potential purchasers of securities are interested in their performance for the investment purposes under consideration. Assessment is relative to the decision-maker's objectives, constraints, quality and quantity of resources. With varying degrees of consciousness, precision, and elaboration, rational profit-oriented evaluation is in terms of the fundamental parameters discussed in § 4.5.

The wide array of securities available should provide the mix of cash income and capital appreciation desired, first through competent selection of individual issues, and second, by their combination in portfolio form. Given the many influences which determine behavior of a security (briefly enumerated in § 5.1) performance of the underlying company is important but not solely determinate.

Growth stocks have become the eagerly sought class, as witnessed by the premium price-earnings ratios they have exhibited for an extended period. This is true for both institutional and individual investors alike, as their reasoning, rational and otherwise, overlaps and is reinforcing. However, relation between growth stocks and growth companies is generally, but not necessarily, direct as noted in § 5.2.

In attempting to identify growth companies, security analysts seek those firms promising superior and continuing increases in earnings per share, safeguarded by complementary trends in sales revenues and physical volume. Furthermore, since innovation often appears primary in sustaining growth, perceived evidence of promising technological research and development can produce an inordinately favorable impression.

Since investor interest in growth stocks is so intense, rewards are great for those who, through detection of a probable uptrend in earnings per share, lead discovery of an incipient growth company. The converse is also true, since a growth company can falter, and those holding its securities may suffer commensurately.

The financial community continuously monitors circumstances likely to affect the behavior of securities. Since, in the case of growth stocks, surveillance is particularly close, financial market response to changes in the underlying business is rapid and often extreme. It is frequently the peculiar market behavior of a growth stock which alerts outsiders to anomalies in the operations of the growth company itself. The coalescence of influences upon security prices is schematically shown in Figure 5.A.

## §5.4  HOMOGENEITY OF RESOURCES

It has been emphasized that a growth company is one which promises, on a continuing basis, superior increases in earnings per share. Also, it was observed in §5.2 that the source of company growth can be external change in the environment and/or internal change from within the firm.

A business entity can be considered as a total social system in microcosm, possessing its own unique set of behavioral, technological, and financial characteristics. Change in this organism can occur in any one or any combination of the firm's current activities, whether in process, product, market, or locale. Similarly, change may be aimed at a specific stage within the spectrum of substance which can be viewed as ranging through the escalating activity levels of maintenance, adjustment, modification, invention, and innovation.

While emphasis may be in a particular direction at a particular time, *sustained progress* requires an effective *pattern* of change encompassing all sectors of the business, and a *degree* of change ranging through the spectrum of substance.

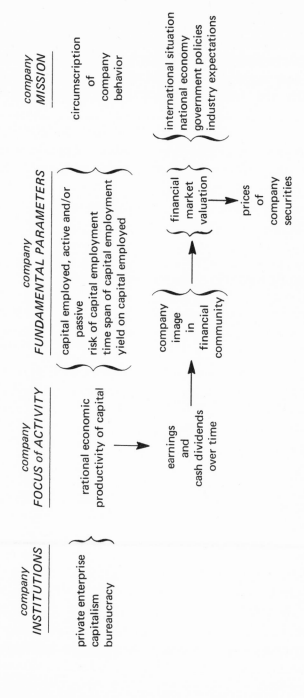

**FIGURE 5.A.  Influences upon Security Prices.**

Thus, sustained superiority in company progress requires strategically astute and *recurrent deployment of resources*, and their expert management once deployed, which in turn presupposes

- company focus on rational economic productivity
- an executive corps which views management as a profession
- emotional detachment toward the process, product, market, and locale being managed
- a sufficiently sophisticated definition of resources to allow identification and allocation on a broad and flexible basis
- a system for planning and implementation universal enough to accommodate, and not restrain, a panoramic degree and pattern of alternatives

Under these circumstances, organization resources are viewed as an *homogeneous pool*, untied to specific endeavors, except by limits in preferences, skills, moral and legal commitments. Even these constraints can become more discretionary with time and effort.

Thus, instead of preserving as sacred the boundaries of process, product, market, and locale, resources become homogeneous by their *transferability* and *transformability* in pursuit of fundamental objectives as phrased in §4.5.


## §5.5  ADVANTAGES AND COMMITMENTS OF GROWTH

It has been concluded that for a large publicly owned U.S. corporation, the most comprehensive single indicator of expected business success is the ratio of common share price to per share earnings.

Superior and continuing increases in earnings can be expected to enlarge the value of the firm's securities in two ways: (1) through the owner's claim on greater assets and earning power, even if the price-earnings ratio remains constant, and (2) by the mounting price-earnings ratio which will probably result from desirability of owning a claim upon this sustained record of success.

As further amplified in §11.1, the sources of preferences orienting organization activities are diverse and changing, compounding the complexity of their detection and reduction into a meaningful whole. In a business, these multiple origins, all *claimants* upon the organization, typically include owners, managers, employees, customers, suppliers, the financial community, relevant professional communities, the government, and society at large.

Aside from directly gratifying one or more of these claimants at any given instant in time, *growth* is often a relatively indisputable objective from a *political* viewpoint. Pursuit of other objectives may require more visible trade-offs between the interests of claimants, sacrificing one for another—if not in all, at least in part. However, growth is more appealing in this respect, some will argue, as all factions supposedly benefit because each gains larger absolute benefit. But, "It ain't necessarily so . . . ." In the fortunate situation where each claimant does in fact gain larger absolute benefit, the relative shares between claimants will almost certainly be altered. Furthermore, opportunities for other benefits will have been lost in the process.

Thus, while these observations should by no means be interpreted as negative toward growth as an objective, it is emphasized that such pursuit may have unpalatable ramifications. On the other hand, the catch-all attractiveness of growth cannot be denied.

Growth can come from external and/or internal means, as discussed earlier. One mode of external growth is through acquisition of interests that control appropriate processes, products, markets, and locales. Their purchase is often, at least in part, a trade for securities of the buying firm. Attractive securities greatly magnify the firm's resource base, in value and form, for external growth through acquisition.

Also, the wide marketability of securities allows founding entrepreneurs great latitude in degree and pace for relinquishing control and gleaning reward through sale of ownership to employees, outside interests, or the public at large.

Thus growth has many advantages for the firm, and these are reflected in its securities. However, continuous growth requires company-wide commitment, competence, effort, discipline, and dedication, coupled with sufficient breadth of perspective and flexibility to view and employ resources as an homogeneous pool throughout the organization. This extremely difficult and rewarding task is facilitated by

- the *institutionalization of profitable change* on a continuing basis, through a comprehensive and formal company-wide planning system
- effective *liaison with the financial community* wherein the strategy and implementation of communication are integral to company-wide planning
- the capacity to *inflict and endure pain* which, in some degree, necessarily accompanies change through dissonance and strain.

The key resource for such a posture is a profit-oriented and professional executive corps seeking excellence in general management, while subordinating and utilizing specialized skills and interests in order to achieve fundamental company-wide objectives.

# CHAPTER 6

# A Concept of Risk

*Ability to find out varies inversely with the need to know.*

—J. M. Birmingham, Jr., C.F.A.

## §6.1 THE NEGLECTED PARAMETER

*Risk* is one of the fundamental parameters established in §4.5. As such, it is inescapable in formulation of preferences which prescribe values and boundaries for subsidiary acts. Consideration of risk is inherent and integral in every management decision.

However, explicit treatment of risk is still rare in business decision-making. In advanced practice, it is usually considered in diffuse and indirect terms as a boundary condition reflected by a minimal yield rate requirement. Ordinarily, it is an intuitive limitation lurking in the recesses of the decision-maker's personal history. And often, risk is all but eclipsed by a simple-minded fixation upon "profit" per se.

Can the intuitive decision-maker cite factors considered in establishing standards for and appraising risk?

Are these applied consistently between one time period and the next? Do all processes, products, markets, and locales receive equal attention in this respect? Are risk appraisals arrived at in different parts of the organization comparable?

Absence of prescription leaves appraisal of risk—and with it important business determinations—to the personal values, limited perceptions, and current emotional status of individual decision-makers.

It is most curious that such a basic company-wide matter as risk is so often sloughed off to that popular receptacle of seeming imponderables, "experience." At best, this constrains activities to the manacles of convention, and at worst, scatters consistency by unconcern. Fortunately, there is little reason for this crippling effect upon pursuit of rational economic productivity to occur.

## §6.2  PREFERENCE AND APPRAISAL

There are two sides to every evaluation of risk, whether explicit or implicit:

1. formulation of *preferences* in general, and
2. appraisal of specific *circumstances* in view of those preferences

As described in §4.1, formulation of preferences is necessary in establishing fundamental objectives, parameters for their expression and implementation, and standards for measurement and control. Company-wide planning recurrently evaluates risk, as indicated earlier and described more fully in Chapters 10 through 15.

The expression and specification of those preferences

particularly pertaining to risk can be made in terms of two simultaneous and parallel dimensions:

1. *probability* of success
2. *confidence* in data

The former is the probability for the estimate of a parameter under scrutiny, while the latter is the reliability accorded factors which determine the probability estimate. Both deal with the future and, as such, are predictions associated with the estimates to which they refer. As predictions, their derivation may be by any appropriate means, ranging from intuition through the use of sophisticated techniques.

The estimates of parameters describing a decision alternative are appraised in regard to both of these dimensions. Should any appear beyond the tolerances specified in these two respects, rejection of the alternative is warranted regardless of benefits otherwise envisioned.

Application of this notion requires a risk appraisal composed of probability and confidence evaluation (1) for each parameter institutionalized in the company-wide planning system, (2) in every interval of the time horizon, short range, intermediate term, and long run, and (3) covering all activities—present, incipient, and proposed.

## §6.3  PROBABILITY AND CONFIDENCE

The selection of dimensions and specification of standards for risk appraisal, and their company-wide enforcement should cast risk considerations into more consistent and precise channels throughout the organization. The two dimensions chosen here, probability and confidence, were sketched in §6.2.

In practice, definition and specification must reflect fundamental preferences of the organization in general, and those pertinent to risk in particular. For illustration, a simple and brief scheme is summarized in Figure 6.A. Here the entire spectrum of risk is trisected into three intervals descriptively termed, from low to high,

1. conservative
2. normal
3. speculative

Such an elementary classification enhances application, as only the polar choices of conservative or speculative need be made—the middle category, normal, being designated by default.

The dual standards for probability and confidence must both be satisfied for an estimate to qualify in a particular risk interval, and every estimate must be assigned to one of the risk classes. Appraisal may assign the probability dimension to one risk class and the confidence dimension to another. A pre-existing protocol, derived from the organization's posture on risk, should determine the disposition in such a case. The options are (1) the probability assignment dominates, or, the confidence assignment dominates, or (2) the highest risk dominates, or, the lowest risk dominates.

Philosophical and logical objections may challenge the degree of mathematical-statistical elegance in this scheme. However, in our opinion, the benefits to be accrued from this type of approach in company-wide awareness and consistency far outweigh the advantages of a more sophisticated but scarcely utilized technique.

If risk is considered, as illustrated, through the parallel aspects of *probability of success* and *confidence in data*, then a decision alternative is to be rejected when its characteristics in either of these respects are deemed beyond tolerable limits.

| CLASS | CONSERVATIVE | NORMAL | SPECULATIVE |
|---|---|---|---|
| **probability requisites** | | | |
| | More than 85 but less than 100 chances of success in 100. | More than 70 but less than 85 chances of success in 100. | More than 50 but less than 70 chances of success in 100. |
| **confidence requisites** | | | |
| information | Quite confident of all estimates due to comprehensive experience in same circumstances. | Fairly confident of most estimates, based upon reasonably complete knowledge. | Little confidence in estimates because of fragmentary knowledge. |
| | Satisfactorily reliable and complete. Routinely available and processed in standard manner. | With some reservations, adequately reliable and complete. Requires some nonroutine selectivity, integration, and synthesis. | Questionably reliable and incomplete. Data preponderantly unavailable and/or unprocessed. |
| techniques | Existing techniques satisfactory. | Some nonroutine analysis and/or modification of existing techniques. | Present techniques untried in new circumstances and/or new techniques. |
| constraints | Acceptance of nondiscretionary constraints, with no contest. | Questioning recognition of nondiscretionary constraints, with some peripheral maneuvering. | Recognition of nondiscretionary constraints, with active confrontation. |

**FIGURE 6.A.   Illustrative Standards for Risk Appraisal.**

## §6.4 AN ILLUSTRATION

This section is intended to demonstrate application of the illustrative risk appraisal scheme in §6.3. An example, brief, simple, and hypothetical, but with sufficient realism to suggest actual usage, will serve to demonstrate the risk appraisal scheme just outlined.

Let us suppose that the core business of a company has been for many years fabrication of mousetraps. In this imaginary case, the manufacturing process commences with the finishing of wood and metal bought from two major suppliers, followed by assembly into several standardized models and sizes, and then packaging. Distribution is to the wholesale level. At retail outlets, the devices are furnished to customers, overwhelmingly night watchmen.

In the mousetrap industry, competition has been clearly oligopolistic, especially in the "high quality" market, but is becoming less so with diffusion of technology, standardization of specifications based upon intended use rather than engineering capability, the price depressing power of institutional buyers including government, and growing sophistication of night watchmen and mice alike.

The short range forecasting of overall demand has been relatively simple, with usage proportional to the population size of humans on the one hand and of mice on the other. Prediction of market share and price is more uncertain, due to accelerating changes in market character noted above, the wider span of types and uses, entry of new materials such as plastic, and impact of more automated production in mousetrap factories.

For our purposes, let us assume that parameters institutionalized for company-wide planning are revenues, costs, and assets employed. Estimates are made for each parameter in terms of physical quantity per time interval under consideration, and these are translated into matching dollar magnitudes for each period. The estimates, physical and dollar, are the most *realistic* which can be made, neither optimistically high nor pessimistically low, but rather *probable* estimates.

Two appraisals of risk are made for each parameter, one for physical quantity and the other for dollar magnitude, per time interval under consideration. The following demonstration of a possible set of outcomes is in context of the summary Figure 6.A, to which reference should be made as required.

Short range revenues, both in terms of physical quantity and dollar magnitude, are rated "conservative." However, intermediate term revenues could be evaluated "normal" because of new competition and shifting market structure, with pricing, and thus dollar magnitudes, more uncertain than physical quantities. Over the long run interval, revenues could be "speculative," given the unknown effects of new pesticide programs by industry and government.

Costs are "conservative" for both the short range and intermediate term, because of the good predictability of physical demand, increasing automation of the fabricating process, and availability of flexible production facilities. Over the long run, however, costs could be "speculative" because of the severely decreased predictability of physical demand, the probable displacement of currently used materials by plastic, and the possible major expansion necessary in production facilities during this time interval. In this case, assets employed would parallel costs, with inventories being the most uncertain variable, especially in the distribution network external to the company.

Profit is a derived parameter, the difference between revenues and costs. Return on assets employed is profit divided by assets employed. What occurs when, for a given time interval, revenues and costs have differing risk ratings, and assets employed still another? In §6.3, some options were noted.

In this example, assume company protocol specifies that the riskiest rating dominates. Then, over the short range, all is "conservative"—revenues, costs, profits, assets employed, and return on assets employed. However, over the intermediate term, because revenues are "normal," while costs and assets employed are "conservative," profit and return on assets employed are both designated "normal." Over the long run interval, all is "speculative."

## §6.5   REFLECTIONS ON RISK

Of the two sides to every risk evaluation, formulation of preferences and appraisal of circumstances, this Chapter focused upon the latter. Discussion of the former is left to §11.1 and §11.2.

In review, estimates are made for each parameter institutionalized by company-wide planning, one for physical quantity and the other for dollar magnitude, in every time interval under consideration. Each such estimate is the most *realistic* which can be made, neither optimistically high nor pessimistically low, but rather a *probable* estimate.

Note the contrast of *probable* estimating with the frequent managerial practice of intentionally understating expected future performance. Often called "conservative," this form of self-protection for the estimator results in underemployment of assets to the detriment of the organization as a whole. Therefore, care must be exercised not to confuse this use of the word "conservative" with our definition.

The scheme for risk appraisal submitted and illustrated in this chapter is intended as a format which may be elaborated and enlarged relative to the circumstances of each case. Definitions for probability and confidence can be tightened, factor checklists expanded, and the number of risk classes increased.

It is stressed that the appraisal of risk, presented here, is unrelated to the magnitude per se of the estimate being assayed for risk. For example, a high profit does not in itself connote low risk. Rather, the designation of risk is based upon the probability of veracity, and reliability of factors determining that probability. In terms of the above example, the high profit could be improbable, and further, the underlying data unreliable, thereby assigning the estimate as high risk.

Nor is one class of risk in and of itself superior to another class. In the wide spectrum of possibilities, the average risk desired in that span, and the permissible distribution around the average, the *risk mix*, are both determined in the formulation of fundamental preferences. For example, suppose it was decided that the average desired risk is "normal": this could be obtained by restricting all ventures to that class, or, specifying a risk mix to achieve this on average; the specified risk mix might even exclude "normal" as a permissible category, relying on purely "conservative" and "speculative" operations.

It should be recognized that risk preference and appraisal are often consequences of the value systems and social institutions characterizing an environment, and the personal histories of decision-makers therein. Individual scope and perception are reflections of this. Thus, in a company diversified by industry and region, an approved framework for risk could be of major import. Does "normal" mean the same to men in the ladies apparel industry as in petroleum refining? Is risk perception the same in the Brazil Division and the Sweden Division?

Commonality and uniformity are necessary concerns in application of every fundamental parameter, including risk. This is underscored if resources are viewed as an homogeneous pool, as amplified in Section 5.4.

In our opinion, the advantages of company-wide awareness and consistency in risk considerations gained through the approach advocated, greatly exceed the disadvantages of objections to elegance by sophisticates. And in any case, the recurrent recycling of the company-wide planning system facilitates adjustment and refinement of preference formulations and the means of appraising circumstances in those terms. The orientation is toward casting risk into more precise and consistent channels, and thus making deployment of resources and their management more effective for the organization as a whole.

# CHAPTER 7

# *A Concept of Time*

## §7.1  ACTIVITY AND TIME

Given the latitudes afforded by nature and society, an individual's discretionary activity is within the bounds of those courses (1) perceived by him as possibilities and (2) deemed compatible with his ongoing and aspired circumstances. The time horizon for both effort and reward, even if intangible and personal, must be within his expected life span.

Man's primary abilities to survive were early enhanced by recognition and application of knowledge regarding periodicity in nature. Thus, it seems reasonable to surmise that seasonality and other cycles in life and land precipitated a first level of time cognizance in man.

With accretion of further insight, these more obvious recurrences have been correlated with patterns in seemingly unrelated phenomena, such as movements of astronomical bodies or decomposition of radioactive materials.

Thus, with increased perception and incentive, a more precise concept of time inextricably develops with the evolution of society. The complexity of this progress, concomitant with that of civilization itself, should not obscure some basic characteristics of time as viewed here:

1. Physical *change is the underlying phenomenon* from which is derived the conventional concept of time.
2. Once the concept of time has developed and stabilized, time itself becomes a *means of measuring* physical activity.

In short, time, in the conventional sense, is a reflection of physical change rather than its cause. And time, as a consequence, becomes one of many convenient measures of physical activity. Therefore, time, because it is common to all, can be used as a parameter to coordinate otherwise heterogeneous activities.

Therefore, given the spectrum of change within which business can be effective, *time* is one of the fundamental parameters established in §4.5. As such, it is inescapable in the formulation of preferences which prescribe values and boundaries for subsidiary acts. Consideration of time is inherent and integral in every management decision.

## §7.2  ORGANIZATION AND TIME

The behavior of individuals and organizations rests upon decision premises in the form of values, facts, and related expectations for the future. These are derived from the relevant culture, society, group, and individual personalities. All have a time dimension. In these respects, the important impact of industry and region qualities has been noted in §4.3.

A particular set of behavioral attributes is coincident with any specific pattern of the above values, facts, and expectations. Other important determinates of economic character are technological and financial criteria—particularly when translated into scale specifications for organization units, and especially during initial resource deployment. Again, each of these criteria exhibits a time dimension.

Time affects individual propensities by its influence upon perception and expectations through such elements as stage of life, career status, and organization rank. In turn, an organization unit acquires a collective time cognition from the composite of behavioral, technological, and financial factors in which its existence rests.

The overall organization necessarily embraces a concept of time accommodating and shaping the agglomeration of decision-making within its components. Further, because of its integrative character, this superordinate entity may operate under a *unique concept of time*, resulting from but different from those of its subordinate units.

Thus the time framework for perception and expectation will differ by individual, industry, and region. Imagine the contrasts in this respect between the ladies apparel and petroleum industries, the Brazil and Sweden Divisions. If components of the same firm, these diverse elements would both influence and be influenced by the company-wide concept of time.

## §7.3 HYPOTHESES ON TIME

The preceding two sections give rise to the following hypotheses toward a concept of time for company-wide planning:

1. The conventional concept of time appears dependent for its development upon a stable and habitually experienced rate, level, and mix of physical activity.
2. A significant change in the foregoing rate or level or mix of physical activity will affect the notion of time with which it is associated.

The implications of these hypotheses permeate fundamental preferences and the consequent avenues for deployment of organization resources and their management.

## §7.4 DEMARCATION AND SEGMENTATION OF THE TIME SPAN

In the conventional view, time is a continuum from the immediate to infinity. For our purposes, the *time horizon* is defined as the point of maximum penetration into the future that is to be considered for the particular activity of interest. Within the span from the immediate to the time horizon, identification and analysis of future periods of concern are aided through segmentation of the span into the number and length of intervals compatible. For instance, one convention, trisection, results in the triad of classic time intervals:

- short range
- intermediate term
- long run

The demarcation of the time horizon and segmentation of the span so defined into intervals is usually intuitive and fuzzy. This is, quite understandable, given the profusion of factors which determines the concept of time. Formal, comprehensive, and company-wide business planning, however, requires uniform and precise definition in the use of this fundamental parameter. This can be accomplished by reference to two factors

- *confidence* in estimates
- *deployability* of resources

Confidence is determined by reliability, which generally decreases the further into the future estimates are considered. So does the ability to implement on schedule the actions ultimately prescribed. The time horizon of each consideration should be terminated where reliabilities of inputs, estimates, or schedules fall below the acceptable level. Tolerance limits may be expressed verbally or perhaps in mathematical-statistical terms. See Chapter 6 for a discussion of explicit treatment of reliability.

And it is recalled from §3.3 that plans for different activities, even within the same organization, may each have a unique time horizon in accord with particular circumstances largely determined by confidence requisites.

To maintain adequate confidence—that is, to keep reliability within desired tolerance limits—time intervals should ordinarily be lengthened with each successive estimate into the future. For example, we have seen that in a given organization, for a ten-year plan, the first year may be in quarterly intervals, the second two years semiannual, the fourth and fifth annual, the sixth and seventh consolidated together, and the eighth, ninth, and tenth years likewise.

Segmentation of the period spanning from the immediate to the time horizon may be achieved with a rationale paralleling the differentiation between operations planning and strategic planning, first offered in §3.6.

- *strategic planning* broadly specifies, on a recurrent basis, preferred means of achieving desired objectives, and is oriented toward deployment of resources
- *operations planning* narrowly specifies, on a recurrent basis, preferred means of implementing strategic plans, and is oriented toward management of resources once deployed

Thus, in terms of the classic triad of time intervals,

- the *short range* is that time interval solely occupied with operations, the management of resources already deployed
- the *intermediate term* is characterized by transition between current and future operations, that is, where resource redeployment has commenced to effect tangible activity
- the *long run*, initiated when resource redeployment has been completed, reflects the full operations impact of the already executed strategy

This trisection has precedent in the economic notion

that all costs are variable in the long run, and that regressively shorter time periods are characterized by commensurately increasing fixed costs. Commitments, whether behavioral, technological, or financial, are stationary until satisfied or dissolved. Prospects for their resolution, and with this, the freeing of underlying resources, increases with time. In a broader and more meaningful way, managerial decision-making generally becomes more discretionary with penetration into the future.

We have suggested that a dual control of confidence and deployability demarks the time horizon and segments the span defined by it. In given circumstances, it could happen that the reliability specified so shortens the time horizon that the long run or even intermediate term are excluded from consideration. Putting it another way, the lower the specified confidence level, the further the time horizon—resulting in a higher probability of including not only short range but intermediate term and perhaps long run as well.

Thus emerges the important recognition that an industry and/or region warrants its own unique time horizon and segmentation of time span, in accord with the flexibility of resource redeployment. Further, the span under consideration may be truncated because of reliability requisites. For example, the absolute time period considered to be "long run" in the ladies apparel industry may be less than short range in petroleum, and likewise, in a comparison of the Brazil and Sweden Divisions. Also, the reliability of estimates in the apparel industry and the Brazil Division may be so wanting as to prohibit a long run interval in their planning.

Obviously, in matters complex and dynamic, demarcation of the time horizon and segmentation of the time span terminated by it cannot be detailed and static. On the contrary, effective utilization of these two dimensions requires precise though broad definition, with revisions as conditions require. This is especially true for the intermediate term, where both internal specification and environmental forecasting are enigmatic.

## §7.5 CONFIDENCE VERSUS ADMINISTRATION

It has been asserted that as the time horizon is extended into the future, reliability, and thus confidence in estimates, generally decreases. Therefore, in considerations of the time parameter when designing a company-wide planning system, two distinct alternatives appear:

1. Specifying *equal confidence* in estimates for all activities can cause to be associated with each activity a unique time horizon and segmentation of the time span so defined.
2. Imposing *equal time horizons* and uniform segmentation of the time span so defined upon all activities can cause unequal confidence to be associated with estimates of each.

A system incorporating the first option will foster technical veracity and sacrifice administrative simplicity. The reverse is true when the second option is selected in system design. For an organization comprised of homogeneous activities, the two design options will be coincident in form and consequences. Choice between the two options becomes paramount when the time parameter is a prime means of coordinating otherwise heterogeneous activities. However, prior simulation of the results contemplated from the pursuit of each option may reveal no significant difference between them, in which case the selection can be made on other grounds.

All other things being equal—and they almost never are—two arguments favor the first alternative, that of system design for equal confidence in all estimates:

1. Confidence measured on the basis of industry and region is likely to engender greater operations support for company-wide planning than enforced adherence to administratively convenient and uniform time horizons and segmentations of the time span.
2. Bureaucracies are ordinarily adverse to risk, and orientation toward equal confidence in estimates offers best prospects for assessment and control.

In an organization characterized by heterogeneous activities, it should be recognized that a company-wide planning system designed for equal confidence in estimates could precipitate administrative chaos through

- unequal time horizons, one for each activity
- segmentation of the time spans so defined into differing intervals for short range, intermediate term, and long run
- possible truncation of one or more intervals from the time span for each activity

The rationale for separation of activities could be with respect to process, product, market, and locale. While division of activities is not the topic of discussion here, it is mentioned as a reminder of the additional intricacies attendant upon this framework with respect to confidence and administration. Clearly, the expected benefits gained through this pursuit of equal confidence in estimates should be sufficiently significant to offset the administrative finesse necessary to counter what will be a tendency toward mechanical snarl.

With this in mind, it is suggested that *initial efforts* in company-wide planning follow the path of administrative simplicity—imposing equal time horizons and uniform segmentation of the time span. In recognizing the possible sacrifice of technical veracity, the selection of this option should be later reviewed, and perhaps reversed, when the necessary sophistication has been reached and the anticipated advantages appear.

# CHAPTER 8

# *A Concept of Resources*

*One man's meat
is another man's poison.*

## §8.1 THE NATURE OF RESOURCES

Since company-wide planning is oriented toward the deployment of resources, this presumes that resources are both (1) identifiable and (2) allocable.

Identification of resources is relative to organization objectives, the processes available for resource transformation, and managerial competence.

- *managerial competence* Has pitchblende been an energy resource to nationals in Republic of the Congo, a major world supplier?
- *processes available for transformation* Is coal an immediate resource in the operation of a nuclear thermal electric generator?
- *organization objectives* Would a new nuclear ther-

mal electric generator be an immediate resource to a small electric utility committed to steady per share earnings increases, especially if debt and dilution are near maximum allowable limits?

What might otherwise be resources may be excluded by the bounds of mission, or even the course of strategy.

- *mission*  Is patent ownership of an effective chemical contraceptive, discovered by chance, a resource as such in an organization restricted by charter to the food industry, and whose owners are opposed on religious grounds to birth control?
- *strategy*  Are excellent financial contacts in Japan a resource for portfolio management by an investment counsel firm whose marketing strategy focuses upon affluent Americans still prejudiced by World War II experiences?

Even if resources are identified as such, the implication is only potential because allocability is a necessary requisite for translation of resources into benefits. This depends on the degree of flexibility in terminating their current application in favor of a new commitment.

- *economic*  When are the resources incarcerated in a half-finished dam allocable to another venture?
- *behavioral*  Following the precedent of airline youth fares, how would the public react to sale, at reduced prices, of unoccupied hotel space, a resource, to unmarried teenagers?

As these examples suggest, the quality and extent of resources can be meaningfully assayed only in view of the ends sought, the means of utilization, and the character of skills available.

As noted previously, the term *resource* alludes to any means through which benefit is derived. In this sense, every factor—actual or potential, tangible or intangible—can be a resource. In this context, it is important to observe that those resources viewed as tangible are ordinarily deemed so on the basis of their relative adaptability to expression through conventional accounting practice.

Resources, even if *identifiable*, may not be administratively *allocable* within the range technologically feasible and economically beneficial. These two restraints, if sufficiently pervasive, will significantly limit the scope of planning and delineation of resources per se. It is also noted in passing that neither benefits nor resources need be necessarily economic, although their differentiation from other forms is not clear-cut, especially when bordering on noneconomic activities.

Thus, in grappling with the concept of resources, their nature will be found to be protean. Suffice it to say here that a resource is one to the extent that it may be transformed from its present status to one desired, within the time span under consideration, and the circumstances expected.

## §8.2 ECONOMIC RESOURCES

The material products of the present are the consequence of past economic activity. Current economic activity evolves two types of products for future utilization:

1. products which, when completed, are *consumed* directly,
2. products which, when completed, are used to *produce* other products

The classification of products in this manner depends upon many considerations, some of which are arbitrary. Examples of the first type would be writing paper, soft drinks, and firecrackers. Dams, blast furnaces, and machine tools typify the second. A diamond, worn as an ornament is the former, and the latter when a cutting tool. Likewise, a television receiver, when used for household entertainment would be in the former category, but, if installed in a factory for quality control surveillance the same equipment could be in the latter group.

In traditional manner, the factors of production are presented in three categories:

- resources from *nature* in fixed supply
- labor from the *human* population
- capital from the *economic* system itself

Conventionally, natural resources and labor are designated the primary factors of production since these are said to be determined largely outside the economic system. On the other hand, capital is considered an intermediate factor of production because it is derived from and for the economic system itself. At best, the dividing lines between these factors are quite hazy. As a natural resource, is the ocean in fixed supply? Is the availability of female labor really divorced from the economic environment? Can a government printing press produce capital?

The context in which economic resources are viewed is, then, greatly influenced by four dimensions:

- the *function* in which they are employed
- the *intent* with which they are applied
- the *conventions* of national accounting
- the *time horizon* within which determinations are considered

Given a truly long run perspective, noneconomic resources may be transformed into those that are economic, and conversely. Also, conversion could and will occur between the classes of economic resources themselves. At this juncture, however, it should be apparent that the terminology regarding resources is imprecise, and, not all economic resources are what is normally called *capital*.

## §8.3  CAPITAL RESOURCES

Having indicated the diffuse nature of resources, and the imprecise terminology used to describe them, this section focuses upon one of the three classic factors of production—capital.

While benefits result through deployment and management of *all* organization resources in concert, by far the most widely used objectives, systems, and standards for business pertain to capital as the ultimate and universal resource, expressed in terms of

- capital *forms* and their array, and
- *changes* in capital forms

Both have a time dimension, but the former is static and the latter dynamic. Capital forms are depicted through a balance sheet, and capital changes via an income statement, perhaps complemented with a funds flow report.

If the firm is itself viewed as an instrument of production, the economic benefits it generates can be thought of as emanating from resources employed in this intermediate entity. With such a perspective, justification can be found for business' concentration upon capital to the virtual exclusion of all other resources.

What does the word "capital" mean. . .equipment or money? Does it ever include natural resources or people? Is it used the same way by economists, politicians, and businessmen? Has the term common definition in highly developed and poor countries. . .within democracies, republics, under socialism, fascism, in communism?

Ranging from subtle differences to real disagreements, the simultaneous universality of the word "capital" and lack of uniformity in the concepts of capital is striking. Yet this seemingly ephemeral capital evidently possesses a core substance which all of modern civilization endorses. Moreover, business the world over pragmatically produces, uses, publishes, discusses, and acts upon balance sheets, income statements, and funds flow reports, and derivatives from all the preceding.

Thus, it is relevant to observe that in an accounting context, an *asset* connotes property in capital resource form, as a money value composed of the sum of ownership and claims thereon, whereas *owners equity* is that asset value less those claims.

So avoiding further entry into the melange over definition, we leave that to the reader and his professional literature, and move on.

## §8.4  VALUATION OF THE ENTERPRISE

As stated earlier, resources are such only in relation to organization objectives, the processes available for resource transformation, and managerial competence. Variances in these three can affect the identity of resources.

While the common concern of all should be the optimum extraction of benefits from the resources in question, the specification of standards for achievement, and thus for resource allocation, depends upon the category of decision-maker. Thus, even in the same circumstance, indices useful for one purpose may not be so in another.

Historically, *owners equity* has been a primary index for the valuation of business enterprise. In the U.S.–with increasing reliability, precision, and consistency in financial reporting–this measure remains most important for companies in situations where market-oriented standards have not been developed. Examples would be privately held firms and companies too unique or small.

In publicly held corporations concentrating upon finance, natural resources, and utilities, *net assets* can be of some valid analytical use. For publicly owned companies, and with some exception for those noted above, there is *little relation* between the *balance sheet accounts* and valuation indicated by *security prices* in financial markets.

Securities of companies characterized by relatively predictable and superior earnings growth tend to sell at premiums related to owners equity, and conversely. This suggests public faith in a connection between current profitability and future growth therein, and the impact of this perception upon security prices. The relationship may be amplified by reference to Figure 5.A.

When securities sell at deep discounts, one possible inference is that the underlying company is "worth more dead than alive." That is, if the firm were dissolved and its assets sold, the aggregate value could be greater than that of the going concern. Or, taking a less drastic viewpoint, the divisions of the company might be more successful operating separately rather than in concert. The reasons for this condition could be many; for example, adverse legal constraints and poor management.

Conversely, when securities sell at high premiums, the investing public feels that prospects for the company are so promising that a price beyond pro rata book value is warranted. For instance, the securities of some "conglomerates" sell not only beyond book value, but at a price greater than would probably be paid for the aggregate of securities from its separate divisions, if these were issued and traded independently. The extra increment, i.e. the premium, could reflect the excellence of corporate-level management, or perhaps resources and administration made available to the divisions, and possibly an advantage afforded by their combination.

## §8.5 MANAGERS VERSUS OWNERS

To the degree that management and ownership are divorced, a potential conflict of interest between the two groups threatens effective utilization of organization resources.

Owners are disadvantaged if greater resources are employed than would otherwise be required for effective operations. On the other hand, managers can be expected to be biased, for reasons of personal security, toward "conservatism"—in reality underemployment of resources. This form of inefficiency would be suggested, but is not necessarily indicated, by the following:

- a capital structure composed only of common stock
- a mode of business operations lacking long term financial commitments
- a high dividend payout relative to earnings and stock price
- excessive working capital, and, inordinate liquidity of assets
- expansion only within the traditional bounds of process, product, market, and locale
- an executive corps exhibiting serious gaps in the thirty to forty age range
- emphasis upon "image" through diffused sales promotion, lavish customer entertainment, or unfocused technological research

In particular, managers deficient in financial sophistication underestimate the costs and risks concomitant with additions to resources already employed in mature activities. Despite the comfort of a well-worn groove, "more of the same" can be inhibiting, obstructive, detrimental, or devastating, in proportion to the permeation of such traditionalism.

Recognizing the nature of resources, their economic context, and universality of capital as the business focus, *capital employed* was established as a fundamental parameter in §4.5. As such, it is inescapable in the formulation of preferences which prescribe values and boundaries for subsidiary acts. Consideration of capital employed is inherent and integral in every business decision.

Furthermore, to emphasize that capital, once deployed, is committed (whether frugally or not) the descriptive phrase *active and/or passive* was added in §4.5.

In order to facilitate resolution of discrepancies between the outlooks of owners and managers, it is appropriate to assign each group mutually supporting, compatible, but differing indices of capital employed:

| *role* | *index of capital employed* |
|--------|------------------------------|
| owner | value of *owners equity*, by market standards if possible |
| manager | *total assets* for which responsible |

While the above two indices scarcely suggest the many indices both current and potential, they do serve to illustrate the need and possible alternatives for multiple measures of the fundamental parameter—capital employed.

# CHAPTER 9

# *A Concept of Productivity*

> *How to have your cake and eat it too: Lend it out at interest.*

## §9.1 THE NOTION OF INVESTMENT

The identification of resources, as amplified in Chapter 8, must be viewed in relation to organization objectives, the processes available for resource transformation, and managerial competence. The same is true for evaluation of *benefits* derived from these resources.

In this framework, *investment* is the present commitment of resources in anticipation of future benefits. Similarly, an *investment operation* is one which, through analytical appraisal, promises the desired benefits with the required degree of confidence. Conversely, if appraisal is nonanalytic, or the benefits not predicted, or the degree of confidence unestimated, the operation is not of investment character. Should resources be employed without expectation of benefit, investment has not occurred. This dictum applies to all circumstances, economic and noneconomic alike. In either case, investment is based upon rationality and is oriented toward gain, private or social. Of course, any evaluation must reflect the indices chosen for measurement.

It has been emphasized that the core of business activity is *rational economic productivity* which requires, for survival and growth, motivation by and satisfaction of profit incentives. It was also observed that business concentrates upon capital resources to the virtual exclusion of all others, expressing this in terms of capital *forms* and their array and *changes* in capital forms—the former reflected in the balance sheet, and the latter by income statement and funds flow report.

Thus, in business, resources and benefits are ultimately approximated and appraised in terms of capital—resources being expressed as capital forms, and benefits as changes in capital forms.

## §9.2 BENEFITS FROM CAPITAL

In §8.2, the factors of production were delineated in traditional manner as (1) resources from nature in fixed supply, (2) labor from the human population, and (3) capital from the economic system itself. The classic benefits to these are rent, wages, and interest.

A primary benefit resulting from employment of capital as a resource, *interest*, has classically been viewed as compensation derived through

- *productivity* gained from employment of capital
- *abstinence* from consuming capital while it is employed
- *uncertainty* inherent in employment of capital

The productivity of capital is a technological phenomenon. Technology is concerned with input, process,
and output in physical terms. The direct application of
given quantities of the two primary factors—natural
resources and human labor—may produce a certain
quantity of finished product. However, if the same
primary factors are applied in part toward the production of the intermediate factor, capital, and if the rest of
the primary factors are then used with the intermediate
factor, even greater quantities of finished product may
be produced than previously. The use of capital is
therefore an indirect process which initially requires
more time than a direct process, but which can have
greater technological productivity.

In order to amass capital, two aspects of abstinence
from current consumption are necessary: (1) the capital
amassed in the past must be left intact; (2) current
activity must be diverted, in part, from the production
of consumption goods to the production of capital
goods. The extent to which this abstinence will be
endured is determined by the desire for current consumption as opposed to the expectation of even greater
future consumption derived from capital invested at the
sacrifice of current consumption.

The commitment of capital for anticipated benefit
requires current deprivation from consumption, and
bypass of other opportunities for its employment. The
estimates surrounding this decision to invest are all
predictions, and as such are subject to uncertainty
inherent in considerations of the future. In formulating
estimates, it is vital to remember that exposure to
uncertainty jeopardizes not only the possible benefits,
but also the resource itself.

## §9.3  YIELD DEFINED AS TOTAL RETURN

In line with business practice, benefits from capital employment can be categorized as to whether they effect

- change in *amount* of capital, or
- change in *form* of capital

Two hypothetical extremes, for example, might be an investment the purpose of which is solely to change the amount of capital—say increase it—without regard to the impact upon its final form. Another investment might be entirely designed to shift the form of capital—to gain liquidity—without limit as to change in total value.

Another rationale is based on sorting the stream of benefits in accord with

- degree of *tangibility*, and
- place in the *time* span

The perceived tangibility of a benefit, and its association with a specific time interval, current or future, will influence the amount and form of capital. Both tangibility and timing are inextricably entwined with accounting practice, legal ramifications, and tax implications.

Whether benefits are considered explicit or implicit, a matter of tangibility, largely reflects national economic philosophy. The distinction between capital gains and income is likewise a convention in which source and timing are relevant. Even realization or nonrealization of capital gains is a purely mechanical phenomenon, generally dependent upon execution of a legally recognizable transaction. The demarcation of short- or long-term gains in the United States is, for example, relative to a purely arbitrary ownership period of six months. The relation between interest and dividends is close, and their differentiation sometimes marginal.

In this same manner, management often perceives "investment" as tangible assets, the legal life of which is longer than one year—while "expense" is either a fixed asset, the life of which is less than one year, or, intangible. When taken literally, the result of such legalism is a narrow, shallow, and short range concept of investment, in which "expense" is viewed almost as a free resource. In this case, the double criteria of tangibility and timing delineates a basic differentiation which can have profound impacts upon effective utilization of resources.

Thus, benefits to capital are classified in accord with their effects upon amount and form of the existing resource base as well as their tangibility and the timing related to national economic philosophy and professional practice. Therefore, unless indicated otherwise, we shall usually view all benefits to capital—regardless of amount, form, tangibility, and timing—as *yield.*

This approach supports the concept of "total return" by weakening procedural barriers to the fundamental comprehension and analysis necessary for rational deployment of resources and their management. However, in particular organizations, and for specific reasons, it may be desirable to separate benefits to capital into two or more classes. As the impetus for this special treatment is likely to be operational, rather than strategic, the prime concept of "total return" should still dominate through the seminal definition of yield offered here.

## §9.4 THE IDEA OF PRESENT VALUE

All economic activity is essentially oriented toward the future. To induce investment, the immediate pleasure of consumption must be subservient to the promise of greater satisfaction from expected benefits.

The one equivalent of all net benefits expected from a specific investment throughout the relevant time span is termed its *present value*. The present value of an investment depends upon

- the expected future *benefits* in amounts expressed as a profile through time, and
- the *yield rate* deemed appropriate to the circumstances

Estimates of benefits should be the most realistic which can be made. The yield rate utilized for calculating present value is a prestated standard associated with the risk category of investment being considered. Classification of risk was discussed in Chapter 6, while development of yield standards is amplified in §9.5, and §11.2.

The present value of a stream of future benefits is determined through an algebraic process which reverses the familiar compounding of interest. Each increment of future benefit is discounted—that is, reduced—to a point in time chosen as the base for analysis, most often the present. These discounted increments of value, all brought to the same point in time, are summed. That aggregate is the present value of the stream of future benefits in question.

If the present value of future benefits equals the present value of resources to be invested, the project will recover the assets committed, and further, provide the specified yield on those assets. If the former is greater than the latter, the yield will exceed that required. This is, of course, desirable. If the latter is greater than the former, the yield will be less than necessary, and the assets committed could be dissipated.

In summary, all other things remaining the same, the present value for a given amount of future benefits decreases (1) as their distribution through time lengthens, or (2) as the specified yield rate increases. The converse is also true; that is, if either the time shortens or the specified yield rate decreases, the present value increases.

For the purpose of this discussion, which is primarily concerned with substance rather than procedure, the preceding description of the present value concept is sufficient. It should be recognized that investment productivity has been and will be measured in many ways other than in terms of present value. The use of other techniques may be justified for specific reasons in particular organizations. These alternate methods, however, are often fragmentary and misleading. They are not so widely applicable, and may lack comparability between different time intervals used for appraisal. Present value, then, will be the means of calculating investment productivity throughout our discussion.

## §9.5   STANDARDS FOR YIELD

A general approach to estimating future financial performance and risk appraisal was described and illustrated in Chapter 6. In review, a dual estimate is made for each parameter institutionalized in company-wide planning—one for physical quantities and the other for dollar magnitudes—in every time interval under consideration. Each estimate is the most realistic which can be made, neither optimistically high nor pessimistically low, i.e., a *probable* estimate.

In accord with the "total return" definition given in §9.3, yield is considered the sum of benefits derived from resources invested relative to the value of those resources. In the usual business context, this is expressed as profit gains from and relative to capital employed.

In ordinary practice, to determine present value yield for a specific investment, estimates would be needed for

- the stream of associated *assets* employed, in both amount and profile, through the time span considered
- the stream of associated *revenues*, in both amount and profile, through the time span considered
- the stream of associated *costs*, in both amount and profile, through the time span considered

In Chapter 6, it was observed that there are two sides to every risk evaluation: formulation of preferences and appraisal of circumstances. The dimensions chosen for the latter were probability and confidence. Adhering to a company protocol for risk appraisal, the investment under consideration would be assigned to a risk class. In terms of the scheme outlined in §6.3 and §6.4, one of three categories would be used, "conservative," "normal," or "speculative."

Within the spectrum of risk deemed allowable by the organization, many possible risk commitments may exist. It was earlier argued that investment opportunities not within this acceptable risk span are to be dismissed from consideration, even if promising in other ways. Of those possibilities still remaining, some will be eliminated because their implementation could skew the *risk mix* undesirably, as was briefly discussed in §6.5.

On this basis, appraisal of investments for risk both filters and sorts those under consideration. Following this, a calculation of yield, by whatever technique, provides a quantitative estimate of investment productivity within the circumstances established as relevant.

Each of the organizations' as yet uncommitted resources is, of course, a potential addition to productivity in general, and to its ultimately assigned risk class in particular.

Our preceding commentary in regard to yield focused upon its estimation and calculation. We now discuss establishment of standards for measurement and control of yield.

Standards should be clearly within the realm of feasibility. Estimation of a *feasible* range for yield must, at least, refer to the following influences, listed in descending order of scope:

1. range of yield feasible in the relevant economy
2. yield spread associated with the host industry
3. effect upon yield of contemplated operating scale
4. yield technologically possible with company facilities
5. impact of allowable product mixes upon yield
6. interplay between management capacities and yields

Once these influences have been estimated, a *probable yield* for each risk class is developed through reference to such aspects as the

- feasible range of yields for the company
- permissible risk span
- specified risk mix
- personnel quality

Each yield rate so developed is paired with its associated risk class. On an overall basis, the average yield desired should be provided by the specified risk mix.

In terms of probability theory, such yield rates are *expected values*. To compensate for statistically anticipated failures, and for motivational purposes, these yield rates could be rephrased for middle management as qualifying requirements to be met for commitment of resources.

For example, below is a set of illustrative yield rates, expected and qualifying, matched with the three risk classes we have been using:

| risk | expected yield rate | qualifying yield rate |
|---|---|---|
| conservative | 17% | 20% |
| normal | 20% | 28% |
| speculative | 25% | 50% |
| specified risk mix | 21% | — |

As noted in §8.5, to accommodate the respective outlooks of owners and managers, it may be appropriate to utilize supporting, compatible, but differing indexes of yield for each. This is similarly so within subcategories of these two groups, in accord with general emphasis and specific purpose. For instance, yield may be computed before or after depreciation, and pre- or post-tax, in accord with special interests. While extended discussion of this type of differentiation of indices is not appropriate here, suitable application of the notion is necessary for successful management.

For each new planning cycle all investments, current and potential, should be classified by risk and evaluated by yield. Resources are allocated to each risk class and then to potential investments in sequential order of declining yields. The interdependence of all preferences and standards, and the iterative process whereby they are derived and refined, should now be apparent.

*Part Three*

# INSTALLATION
# OF
# THE SYSTEM

# CHAPTER 10

# *Establishing Commonality*

> *Today's right questions*
> *are to be desired*
> *over yesterday's right answers.*
> —Attributed to Leonardo da Vinci

## § 10.1 SELECTION FROM THE COMPANY VIEWPOINT

Some revealing answers to critical questions must be developed before the chief planner is engaged. These queries, of two types, are addressed first from the company viewpoint in § 10.1, and then from the chief planner's in § 10.2. The responses to one set of probes actively affect the other.

Is the firm sufficiently acquainted with the concept and ramifications of formal, company-wide, and comprehensive business planning to decide intelligently if this function is truly desired? To specify the type of planning desired? To effectively host such a function throughout the organization?

Does the company wish, in fact, to establish "plan-

*107*

ning" to cover another operation poorly performed but politically sacrosanct? If true planning is desired, is it to be topic or technique oriented? Nonrecurrent by project or recurrent through a system? Strategic, for deployment of resources, or operational, for management of resources once deployed?

What degree of authority is the planner to be allowed regarding his function and beyond? for concept? substance? format? procedure? scheduling? quality control? assumptions and constraints for each planning cycle? development of process, product, market, and locale? acquisitions and divestments? At what levels will this authority operate?

How much activity external to the firm is the planner to engage in? recruiting his subordinates? peers? their subordinates? Dealing with outside consultants? Consulting with customers? Representing the company in professional societies? academic circles? trade organizations? to the government? Conducting financial community relations? Strategy or liaison? Acquisition and divestment search? Negotiation? At what levels will he engage in such activities?

What is intended as the planner's ultimate fate? Line or staff or out? If line, Division Operations or the Presidency? If staff, lateral transfer to another function or promotion as chief of all staff services? If out, in what style? As a director? In a sinecure? Pawned off to another firm? Or terminated without recourse upon completion of pre-agreed tasks?

From the company viewpoint, the profile derived from these inquiries should determine basic personnel specifications for the chief planner. Is he to be a brilliant and innovative conceptualizer? a strategist? an entrepreneur? Expert in a particular industry or management function? Experienced in operations? Primarily a politician? The human relations type? A colorless administrator? Or a namby-pamby passive coordinator? Possibly a step-and-fetch-it boy? Maybe a fall-guy? Which age range and career stage? What combination and weighting of these characteristics is desired? How much is this package worth to the company?

For maximum effectiveness in company-wide planning and in fairness to all concerned, these questions should be resolved completely as possible upon engagement of the chief planner. The answers and uncertainties should be frankly discussed with candidates, for advice and accord. To do otherwise would be both wasteful and unethical.

Let us assume that the company has rationally decided to develop the formal, comprehensive, and company-wide planning system described, and, that it is seriously searching for and preparing to effectively host the competent professional planner who will direct its conceptualization, installation, and operation.

## § 10.2 SELECTION FROM THE PLANNER'S VIEWPOINT

The planner in turn solicits and perhaps forces the company to answer the questions just posed; in addition, he should have many answers and opinions of his own.

From a personal viewpoint, is the candidate more interested in professional development, application of skills already possessed, a particular organizational environment, remuneration, or the geographic location?

With respect to career aspirations, is the company characterized by an appropriate industry, size, and stage of evolution? Is the latter basal, growth, maturity, decline, or senility? Concerning professional development, does the position offer a desirable mix of potential experience, exposure, recognition, and visibility?

Looking more closely at the organization, are its behavioral, technological, and financial characteristics compatible with his objectives, constraints, and resources? Is the executive corps a highly stratified old-school-tie club, or a heterogeneous group of aggressive second-generation Americans? Are they complacent conservators or innovative builders? Is the core technology a traditional and simple process or rapidly progressing, sophisticated, and multiple? Is company financing staid and simple, or a volatile conglomeration of assets?

The level of management sophistication is extraordinarily relevant for the prospective chief planner. Is the company family-owned, starting from scratch regarding management as a profession? Is it a well developed functional organization but with no central planning? Or is the planning function to consist of refining an already installed system which extends through group echelons to their subordinate profit-centers?

Depending upon the foregoing, is the chief planner to be a teacher? Conceptualizer? Administrator? Peacemaker? Handholder? Are there topics too sacrosanct for him to probe? Or is he to be ignored except when summoned for image purposes as an "expert"?

In §3.4, the structural position of the chief planner was examined. For many reasons cited therein, direct staff relation to the chief executive is preferred under all but exceptional conditions. The planner's slated superior, as a pivotal figure to the candidate, should be probed with the greatest preparation, scope, and depth. Is communication with him easy? Does he understand? Has he shown related achievement? Does he really care about planning? Can he inflict and endure the pain of change? Can he back innovation? Will he act? Powerfully? Consistently? Who will dominate, the planner, or his superior? In brief, will the de facto relation be support-ive? Complementary, rival, or substitute?

The potential chief planner must decide whether the circumstances are appropriate for *his* unique set of objectives, constraints, and resources. Is the situation compatible now? Within the organization during the future? As a stepping-stone elsewhere in the company or outside?

In general, is the reward worth the risk, however measured? The candidate should bend all efforts to arrive at a rational evaluation, and his persistence in these regards will be of unusual service, not only to himself, but more so, to his prospective employer.

Let us assume that the candidate is a competent professional planner satisfied that the company's circum-stances and intentions appear sufficiently compatible with his own to merit further investigation.

## § 10.3  INITIAL EXPOSURE

Though the variations are many, the following out-lines a sequence of interactions which could initially occur between the candidate for chief planner and the host company. In this sequence, it is assumed that his role is in staff relation to the chief executive, as described in § 3.4.

The reciprocal exploration between the planner and host company may commence through an intermediary, perhaps an independent executive recuiter or "head-hunter." During the several earlier conversations and personal probings which occur, many of the basic questions previously posed should be resolved, perhaps by referral to the as yet undisclosed company. Consequently, an initial meeting is arranged between the three principals—the candidate, the intermediary, and the chief executive—at which time personal interaction commences. Those proceedings are, of course, usually kept in confidence for the protection of all concerned.

If genuine interest is demonstrated by both sides, the negotiations progress with the candidate's visit to company headquarters. In addition to further discussion with the chief executive, he may be asked to meet directors and peers. For this occasion, the planner may decide to offer a formal presentation of his concepts, philosophies, techniques, and modes of operations in business planning (1) to bare himself for scrutiny, and (2) to evaluate his audience through their reactions.

If the planner and his hosts retain their enthusiasm, correspondence should indicate the dimensions of the planning function, a job description and conditions of employment. During this phase, another visit to the company is appropriate, not only with the chief executive, but also to chat with middle management and to tour facilities. Simultaneously, perhaps the planner's wife would survey the situation from her viewpoint.

Much can be learned by observing the behavior of all parties as exploration metamorphoses into negotiation. Managerial competence, technical knowledge, political pressures, ethical and moral fiber are all exposed to view.

A high degree of precision and documentation are to be desired because company-wide planning—as a functional area of management—lacks precedent and requires commitment. It cannot bask in the relative informality of the traditional functions, the particulars of which are well prescribed by custom. Thus, there is no better indicator of comprehension and intent than two-way correspondence.

If either party considers it necessary or useful, these transactions may be monitored by their respective attorneys. Such professional guidance helps clarify conditions and terminology, can widen the span of options, preserve cordiality between principals through third party negotiations, and, safeguard rights and privileges.

Unless exceptional evidence can be presented to the contrary, refusal by the company to reduce commitments to written contract is extremely suspect and extraordinarily risky to the potential incumbent in his very sensitive role of chief planner. This should suggest, to the candidate, an insufficient level of company conviction in the importance and tenure of the planning function and/or himself as its chief, to warrant further contact.

After reaching agreement, a third visit to company headquarters is desirable, this time to undergo routine personnel processing. At this point, more extensive interaction may occur with middle management through a presentation on the planning function similar to the one previously offered to top management. Among other things, this should help to mitigate curiosities and anxieties in that echelon.

At about this time, announcement of the planner's impending employment is made. Internal memoranda should, as a courtesy, precede public announcement by several days. The content and form, wording and distribution, are all important. Through such nuances, parties likely to be affected interpret the degree of authority and responsibility to be associated with the new incumbent. This structures their receptivity, hospitality, and cooperation. Should the chief executive delegate the announcement as a chore, say through the company Secretary, the planning function has been initiated with a whimper that presages its fragile future.

Upon arrival, the newly employed chief planner might be cloistered by his superior, the chief executive, to design his best possible entree to the organization. Following this, the chief executive—to visibly demonstrate strong endorsement—should personally introduce the planner to appropriate personnel at all levels. The planner can then withdraw to study written material for orientation, and to establish residence.

This section described the typically desirable sequence of interactions between the chief planner and the host organization, from initial contact through recruitment and arrival. While prescription was not intended, the importance of this phase—as a foundation for both parties—cannot be underestimated.

## §10.4 DE FACTO STATUS

This first task of the chief planner is to determine the *de facto*, i.e., actual, *decision-making character* of the organization through

- description of de facto *objectives*
- specification of de facto *constraints*

- identification of de facto *resources*
- depiction of de facto *data flow*
- portrayal of de facto *planning*

As might be expected, de facto decision-making will not coincide with that specified by the organization manual and other such guides because of their procedural emphasis and coverage, and normal departures in enforcement of their contents.

The composite of the above factors will imply the de facto *degree* and *pattern* of decision-making *discretion* throughout the organization by process, product, market, and locale. This profile, in turn, delineates the de facto *power structure*.

Because the methods by which determination and description of the *de facto status* may be accomplished are not the subject of this book, they will not be extensively elaborated. In brief, however, they focus upon organization and financial analysis, through (1) a priori study, followed by (2) interviews with relevant decision-makers, then (3) integration and synthesis of the preceding, and finally (4) critique by the management echelon responsible. Suffice it to say that this activity should be at a level of sophistication and detail commensurate with the stage of evolution and management competence of the organization. The time and cost to be devoted is determined by the reservoir of past studies of this type, and payoff anticipated from the prospective undertaking.

For example, the foundation of such work could be a normative model based upon the conceptual framework provided in Chapters 2 through 9, tempered by orientation on the organization and its environment. The de facto status would be described in terms of and relative to, this normative model. Analysis of discrepancies between actual and standard will afford conclusions on (1) the efficacy of the model, (2) the veracity of the description, and (3) the ultimate adjustment of each to furnish a meaningful whole.

As a first effort, the most appropriate approach could be a conceptual overview concerned with substantive matters and macrostructure, while successive studies would be increasingly procedural penetrations of technique and detail.

In consonance with the substantive nature of this first effort, most interviewing and all review should, in that phase, be confined to the topmost management council. As successive studies become increasingly procedural, participation descends into the organization hierarchy. In any case, for veracity, rapport, and credibility, it is essential that the management echelon responsible intensively criticize each such study prior to its completion. And further, it is important that these reviews be utilized and acknowledged as an indispensable contribution to perception and ultimate implementation.

With this approach in mind, the purpose of determining and describing the de facto status is fourfold:

- to derive and present an agreed-upon portrait of the organization in its totality
- to orientate the chief planner to this environment
- to acquaint the host organization with the planning function and its chief
- to precipitate corrective action through the impersonal medium of group dissatisfaction with the portrait presented

In summary, the de facto status, if accepted, establishes a uniform foundation for planning and precipitates corrective action by the management. Because of the substantive nature of this first effort, most interviewing and all review should be confined to the topmost management council. Skillful, sincere, and apolitical execution of this phase will be crucial for the success of all future company-wide planning.

## §10.5  RECOGNIZED NEEDS

The corrective action precipitated by dissatisfaction with the portrait of de facto status is usually either

- elimination of the planning function and its chief, or
- elimination of the unsatisfactory discrepancies

The first alternative will not erase underlying causes or symptoms. However, it does remove the apparent focal point of dissonance and strain, and spare the chief executive from enduring and inflicting the pain of change. Such delay trades aggressive advancement for pleasant harmony by "passing the buck" into the future and to subsequent managers. It is desirable here to assume that the second alternative is chosen, if only to justify reading the remainder of this volume.

Based upon the defacto status, it will ordinarily be obvious at this stage that improvements are crucial in both of two interrelated areas:

- specification of objectives, constraints, and resources, and
- design and operation of the company-wide planning system.

While the second is substantively dependent upon the first, the phrasing of, boundaries for, and standards in the first are procedurally dependent on the second. This circular interdependency suggests both the difficulty of remedial action and the desirability of a pragmatic approach. When such a positive course is embarked upon, the *formative period* of company-wide planning has commenced.

# CHAPTER 11

# *The Formative Period*

> What is the use of a house if you haven't
> got a tolerable planet to put it upon?
> —Henry David Thoreau

## §11.1 IDENTIFICATION OF PREFERENCES

A paramount phase of the planning process is *detection of preferences and their reduction* to a clear, precise, and formal statement, with due regard for priority ordering and consistency. As in all aspects of meaningful planning, it is necessary that this statement be periodically reviewed, both as to prescription and depiction. Since, in an achievement-oriented framework, all else follows from such a focus, this crucial step is both the most *fundamental* and *difficult* in the entire planning function.

Formulated preferences provide values and boundaries for all subsidiary acts, and as such are the *fundamental* determinants of all substantive endeavors. *Difficulty* derives from the underlying demand for a combination of rationality and commitment which appears abnormal in human behavior.

Organized man seems to demonstrate a propensity for risk-hedging and ambiguity, and, a corollary avoidance of performance appraisal. For example, it was earlier pointed out that managers can be expected to be biased, for reasons of personal security, toward "conservatism," which is, in effect, an underemployment of resources. In general, uncertainty regarding objectives, constraints, and resources erodes the basis for discretionary decision-making. In subordinates this replaces the potential of aggressive implementation with passive dependency.

To deploy organization resources and manage them, preferences must be detected and reduced to a form which facilitates planning and implementation for their achievement. Whether they are accomplished implicitly by indirection, or explicitly by system is also, to some extent, a manifestation of preference regarding organization style. In all but the simplest and most static of circumstances, extensive informality is likely to be eclipsed as a desirable alternative by the continuing pressures for superior performance. This is especially so for large publicly owned U.S. corporations whose performance is evaluated by the financial community continuously, and reflected openly in the prices of company securities.

The sources of preferences are diverse and changing, compounding the complexity of their detection and reduction into a meaningful whole. These *claimants* upon the organization—each representing a unique array of desires—are typically for a business:

- *owners* of the company
- *managers* of the company
- *employees* of the company

- *customers* of the company
- *suppliers* of the company
- the *financial community*
- relevant *professional communities*
- the *government*
- *society* at large

Who are the claimants? Which should be officially recognized? Are they to be treated with equality?

Recognition and classification of relevant claimants are, in part, dependent upon value premises. Within this context, specific identification of claimants may require skillful investigation. Extraction and recording of de facto preferences from each claimant rest upon research competence and administrative organization. The aggregation of these diverse preferences is fraught with further value judgements and methodological pitfalls. And, once derived, the content and weighting of these preferences change with shifts in environmental character, organization attributes, and claimant composition.

Faced with such formidable barriers, is it possible to detect and reduce preferences in a manner useful for planning? The answer is obviously affirmative, because planning has been done, decisions made, and actions implemented throughout history.

Satisfaction of preferences is a political phenomenon. The derivation, structuring, and employment of political power has long been a prime focus of study and application in society. What should be the degrees of explicitness, sophistication, and detail in the expression of preferences in any given situation? The answer must rest with a cost/benefit evaluation, even if done intuitively.

Data for a clear, precise, and formal statement of

preferences is initially collected coincident with documentation of the de facto status. Upon this foundation, efforts to better detect and reduce preferences to a more meaningful whole may be extended by such techniques as

- analysis of past behavior of claimants
- informal interviews with claimants
- motivation research on claimants
- formal surveys of claimant groups
- simulated decision-making by claimants

## §11.2  SIMULATION BY MANAGEMENT

The military has long had its war games, and little girls play house. Both are examples of simulation—an exercise of decision-making—through use of a representation in which the subject resources are neither expended nor jeopardized. The focus of the exercise, its degree of realism, and the techniques employed, are all dependent upon purpose, state of the art, and envisioned costs and benefits. There are two major uses for simulation:

- *training* personnel by simulation of known circumstances
- *research* by simulation of hypothesized circumstances

The latter will be the context in which this section is written.

The determination and description of de facto status, amplified in §10.4, will precipitate recognition of needed improvement in specification of objectives, constraints, and resources, as cited in §10.5. Next, the de facto objectives, constraints, and resources are initially identified, analyzed, and phrased by the planner in a manner which tentatively appears more rational, systematic, and consistent than previously.

Then, assuming these tentatively identified objectives, constraints, and resources within a realistically hypothesized environment, organization performance is estimated over the relevant time span. For a business, these estimates are in terms of the fundamental parameters established in §4.5, and are ultimately expressed, as justified in §8.3, as

- capital forms and their array, and
- changes in capital forms

By altering definition, substance, and priority within the several realistically hypothesized environments, an acceptable range of objectives, constraints, and resources can be derived to result in the simulation of satisfactory performance.

This iterated *simulation*, even when very simple and extremely crude, can aid management immeasurably in

- exposing *feasible* sets of objectives, constraints, and resources, and
- reducing these to a few *satisfactory* sets

Thus, the area of ultimate decision is ever narrowly circumscribed in a rational, systematic, and consistent manner by successive simulations. In each simulation, the final set of objectives, constraints, and resources is chosen by application of management judgement and prerogative. The process is repeated until satisfactory performance is simulated.

In the *formative period* of company-wide planning, the simulation described is engaged in only by *topmost management*, with instigation and technical direction by the chief planner. However, in subsequent planning cycles, simulation could be useful throughout the organization, in each hierarchical echelon and sector.

## § 11.3  FACILITATED IMPROVEMENTS

Once objectives, constraints, and resources have been identified, analyzed, and phrased—even if tentatively and crudely—improvements can be rapidly reflected in

- appraisal of *current status*
- *coordination* of present activities
- *estimates* of future potential

Why? In the simulation just described, (1) parameters for measurement and control were defined, (2) priorities were specified between them, (3) a standard value for each was developed, and (4) organization activities were circumscribed by boundaries.

This formalization prescribes indices for evaluation, and discusses their relative importance. Lesser elements may be relegated to their appropriate subordinate status. In short, attention can more readily be focused upon matters of significance, now that differentiation has been made.

For example, the fundamental parameters of §4.5 may have been defined, approved, and endorsed with operational dimensions. Perhaps highest priority was ascribed to stability of asset value, with income and earnings growth following in that order. The implication could be that absolute volume in sales revenues and physical units must be preserved, taking precedence over growth of a volatile nature. And, as a risk aversion, activities must not venture beyond traditional bounds.

Pursuing this illustration, appraisal of current status would emphasize the collection, processing, and analysis of intelligence regarding factors affecting change of assets, with stress upon protection from downside risk. Coordination of present activities would shift toward control of those factors. Estimate of future potential would focus upon the conditions underlying behavior and manipulation of the determinant factors, rather than the totality of that vast panorama called "the future."

In this way, the certainty of formality and documentation replaces the uncertainty of ambiguity and hearsay. License to concentrate upon desired achievement displaces dispersal of resources through management's risk-hedging. Therefore, relative to the specified objectives, constraints, and resources, effective performance is made more probable.

## §11.4  OUTLINE FOR STRATEGY

The process just described—that of identification, analysis, and phrasing of objectives, constraints, and resources—congruently outlines the dimensions of strategy.

*Strategy* broadly specifies preferred means of achieving desired objectives, and is oriented toward *deployment* of resources.

*Strategy-making* requires knowledge of the external environment, establishment of parameters for objectives and standard values for them, and identification of resources and their allocability. Further, missions and policies must be responsive to these for effective deployment of resources.

Even if tentative and crude, the simulation of § 11.2 formalized definition and valuation of underlying parameters and their boundaries. Knowledge of the environment enhanced in pursuit of improvements discussed in § 11.3, namely, appraisal of current status and estimates of future potentials.

In determining and describing de facto status, and then through subsequent simulation, constraints were identified and refined. As the prime discretionary constraint, *mission* prescribes the bounds for organization activities in two dimensions by delineating *scope* and *depth*. The element of time is implied in each. Scope pertains to the lateral range of product and market activities. Depth applies to the vertical range of activities, forward toward customers and backward toward suppliers.

Development of the mission statement and its change through time results from consideration of three major influences:

- *preferences of claimants* upon the organization
- feasibilities afforded by the *external environment*
- *attributes and deficiencies* of the organization, in these contexts

These influences were initially determined and described in their current form via study of the de facto status. They were then simulated in possible future forms, to suggest those combinations most likely to result in satisfactory performance.

Absence of a serious and useful mission statement can result in (1) preservation of the status quo, by default and/or (2) unwarranted dispersal of resources, through political compromise and protective risk-hedging for the security of managers. On the other hand, a rationally developed and extensively communicated mission will encourage concentration of efforts and maximum employment of resources.

Thus, the mission rests upon a melding of the three cited major influences, present and future. From within the framework of an analytically circumscribed zone of feasibility, the final statement is a creatively derived channel for organization activities.

Within the context of mission, policy helps guide activities through clarifying

- approved *preferences* for value judgements
- standard *interpretations* concerning significant and oft-encountered intangibles
- *priority* orders for strategies frequently conflicting

Thus, *policy-making* is the development of *decision rules* for substantive matters, to be applied by appropriate translations at each level in the organization hierarchy. It is not, however, the writing of procedural regulations so often concerned with the trivia of routine.

Unfortunately, policy is typically developed on an ad hoc, uncoordinated, and last-resort basis, normally informal and undocumented, except for legal matters. To the extent that this occurs, traditionalism is reinforced, unfortunately, and the most effective use of resources is prohibited.

## § 11.5  THE PRE-CYCLE PROGRAM

The time interval following determination and description of de facto status and ending with commencement of the first planning cycle is termed herein the *formative period* of company-wide planning.

Thus far, the planning function may appear a mélange of circular and interdependent facets with the progress of each based on advancements elsewhere in the function. However, sufficient development has occurred by this time to enable establishment of a *pre-cycle program* for implementation prior to commencement of the first planning cycle. Its purpose is to:

- *identify areas* of compelling need
- *determine tasks* to be performed in remedy
- *assign responsibility* for their execution
- *budget* the company-wide planning effort
- *segment* the effort into controllable phases

The chief planner must derive, design, and submit the pre-cycle program. Its preparation and presentation should be characterized by all the professional skill and political finesse possible, as the reactions to it will determine the entire future of company-wide planning.

To obtain advice and support for company-wide planning, an appropriately composed *Corporate Planning Committee* of top level executives should be proposed in the pre-cycle program, bearing a limited membership representing every major organization unit and political faction. This committee unit is further discussed in § 12.1.

Often, because of naïvete and eagerness, top management will force the chief planner to act before sufficient orientation, conceptualization, information collection, and analysis have occurred. While an aura of congeniality still surrounds his recent arrival, the chief planner may wish to solidify this ephemeral advantage through gaining commitments for funding and staff. However, even when pushed into premature exposure, his vocational experience, technical expertise, and sensitive perception should afford ample background to author the basic pre-cycle program and its particular adaptation to the circumstances at hand.

Presentation of the proposed pre-cycle program should be made first to the organization's power elite, whomever they are, possibly even through meetings on an individual basis, if desirable to effect communication and interchange at a fitting level of sophistication and security.

Following this, the pre-cycle program, with appropriate modifications, may be offered to the Board of Directors, then to the topmost management council, and next to middle management. Also, the presentation may be given for major owners not represented in any of these groups. Every step downward in the hierarchy requires approval from above, and suitable translation of concept, language, and demeanor.

During this process, it may become apparent that the objectives, constraints, and resources perceived by the organization are incompatible with those of the chief planner. Early recognition of this will have served all concerned in good stead, upon which redirection and/or departure of the chief planner is desirable. However, the probability of this occurrence should have been significantly reduced by care in mutual selection of planner and company.

For the purpose of this text, it is assumed that the pre-cycle program is accepted and approved by all relevant groups. An illustrative pre-cycle program for an hypothetical organization is shown in Figure 11.A.

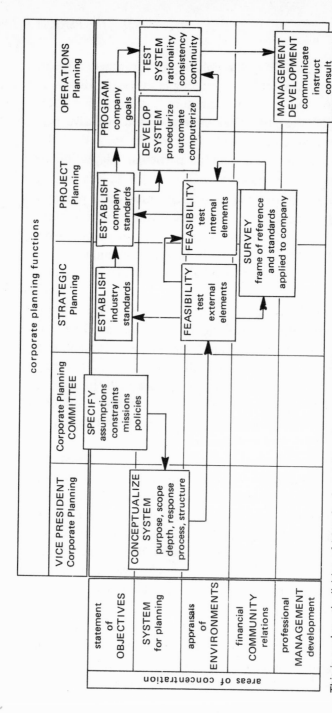

**FIGURE 11.A. Illustrative Pre-cycle Program.**

This is a schematic division of labor for foundation of a company-wide planning system. It is intended to depict areas of concentration and interrelations with relevant Corporate Planning functions. There is no attempt to represent the company-wide planning process beyond this foundation stage, nor to detail the programming and interphasing of that which is presented.

# CHAPTER 12

# *Familiarization*

*Try not to appear as a Space-Age Don Quixote
tilting over traditional windmills*
—A. E. Killeen, Vice President
The Coca-Cola Export Corporation
Johannesburg, South Africa

## § 12.1 THE CORPORATE PLANNING COMMITTEE

The Corporate Planning Committee, as proposed by the chief planner in the pre-cycle program, is the vehicle whereby appropriate high-ranking personnel maintain interest, comprehension, and participation in company-wide planning. Chaired by the chief planner, the Committee would recurrently

- endorse *assumptions*
- suggest *constraints*
- propose *missions*
- develop *policies*

before their submission by the chief planner to his immediate superior, the chief executive. *Guidance provided by the Committee* to the chief planner would focus upon

- *behavioral* aspects of the organization
- *characteristics* of the business
- identification and interests of *power blocs*
- best utilization of *administrative* systems
- location of *expertise* within the organization
- *external contacts* of relevance
- *timing and content* of requests

The Committee would provide support for company-wide planning concomitant with these foci, including desirable entrees to relevant groups, and backed by resource allocation to the company-wide planning function *per se* from the respective organization units directed by Committee members. Especially during the pre-cycle program, this support should stimulate an array of subsidiary assignments from Committee members to their subordinates. The Corporate Planning Committee also serves to orient and educate in at least four ways:

- Committee members become acquainted with concepts, philosophies, and techniques of company-wide planning.
- The chief planner becomes acquainted with the internal feasibilities and behavioral characteristics of the organization.
- Committee members sense and probe the capacities and motivations of the chief planner.
- The Committee, because of its substantive and multifunction deliberations, is an outstanding mechanism for top management development.

In view of its purposes and impacts, the Committee should be small enough to facilitate its members' effective participation and contribution, and yet of sufficient size to accommodate all significant sectors and political factions. The former is necessary for ease of communication and free interchange at a fitting level of sophistication and security. The latter is desirable, not only for appropriate guidance and support, but also for timely and credible dissemination of planning-related information to the remaining organization—both formally and through "the grapevine." Any difficulties underlying satisfaction of these Committee functions, either in organization structure or staffing, could suggest more basic changes later on.

Thus, the selection of Committee members and their serious participation are critical for both the technical functioning of company-wide planning and its political virility. Every effort should be made to imbue Committee existence with utmost import, its body with prestige, and its deliberations with authority. Development of this status commences with inclusion of the chief executive and his visible participation thereafter. Within context of the role described, an illustrative Committee roster could be

- chief planner, chairman
- chief executive, senior member
- Executive Vice President, member
- Vice President for Finance, member
- Vice President in charge of Group A, member
- Vice President in charge of Group B, member
- Vice President in charge of Group C, member

## § 12.2 A BRIEF GLOSSARY OF PLANNING TERMS

Assuming the organization and staffing of such a Corporate Planning Committee, its first task would be guidance and support for the pre-cycle program. Without question, definition and standardization of terminology will be required at this juncture to develop company-wide planning activities throughout the organization. Following are definitions of simultaneously important and frequently used planning terms:

An *estimate* is a conditional forecast expressed in terms of approved parameters and their standard values.

Any *conditional forecast* has as its dual bases (1) a precisely hypothesized environment within which (2) a specified set of activity-oriented premises are pursued.

Particulars regarding the hypothesized environment, and specifics for the set of activity premises, whether explicit or not, exist. Therefore, rather than act on obscure implication, the assumption underlying each should be formalized as desirable to achieve understanding and facilitate subsequent surveillance for departure from them.

There are various types of *estimates*, each a form of conditional forecast characterized by its own combination of technical sophistication and economic cost, some of which are defined below.

**trend**  an *indication* of a prevailing magnitude, direction, and rate of change, necessarily historic, and dependent upon the quality of data and time period chosen

**extrapolation**  an *extension* of a trend, inferring its continuance, and suggesting the underlying, naive, and unlikely assumption that all other things remain equal

**projection** a systematic *presentation* of a partially subjective estimate, relying heavily upon extrapolation, modified for explicit assumptions other than maintenance of the status quo

**forecast** a *prediction* of future conditions, for which all major assumptions are explicit and consistent, based upon (1) a *realistically* hypothesized environment, and (2) specified premises regarding the particular activity of interest. Note that the specified premises may consist in whole or in part of an approved plan, program, or budget.

The above categories of estimates have been listed in order of escalating explicitness and realism. These two criteria should not be confused with technological sophistication in the development of estimates or refinement of the estimates themselves. Superiority of any particular form of estimate is determined only in relation to the purposes for which it is intended.

Three terms, *objectives*, *goals*, and *conditions* are loosely related and often used interchangeably. However, their differentiation in definition and application can serve significantly to dispel confusion and add sensitivity to communication and analysis in company-wide planning.

**objective** a broad aim or ultimate end toward which a plan is designed and implemented

**goal** a specified achievement, supporting a superordinate objective, measurable at a scheduled point in time, toward which a program is designed and implemented

**condition**  a premise upon whose fulfillment implementation of a plan or program rests, or the
veracity of an estimate is founded

In a broad sense, the three preceding terms, *objective*, *goal*, and *condition*, are listed in increasing order of
specificity and measurability coupled with a decreasing
secular, i.e., long run impact.
Another source of confusion can be the differentiation between plans, programs and budgets.

**plan**  a statement of mutually consistent objectives,
constraints, and resources supported by a comprehensive set of programs and budgets for action and
control in the future
**program**  a set of specified actions designed to
achieve the goals associated with them, and scheduled for execution in the future
**budget**  an operations plan expressly for coordination
of resource acquisition and use, reflecting the
comprehensive plan and particular program governing it, and generally focusing upon the short range
interval

In summary, *estimates* of all types are utilized in
design of plans, programs, and budgets. A particular form
of estimate, *forecasts,* are made before development of
an activity to appraise its need, and during simulation of
the proposal to evaluate its potential effectiveness.
*Budgets* are assembled to support *programs* which, in
turn, are subordinate to *plans.* All are ultimately oriented
toward the attainment of broad aims, *objectives,* through
specific achievements, *goals,* under stipulated premises,
*conditions.*

## § 12.3 FIRST VISIT TO THE FIELD

With approval of the pre-cycle program and organization of the Corporate Planning Committee, the chief planner has completed basal conceptualization and structuring of his function, and apparently has gained demonstrated top management support for it.

The very nature of this phase, however, has required his continued presence at headquarters. During this period, reference has often been made by superiors, peers, and subordinates, to "the field" as a prime source of productivity, influence, and innovation. That almost universal colloquialism, "the field," refers to any echelon below headquarters, usually operations oriented, and often geographically removed.

Behaviorally "the field" is, along with other things, a generator of company folklore, and a major repository thereof. It is a training ground and Alma Mater, legitimizing its graduates, and providing them with a thread of commonality excluding others not so blessed. For these reasons, it can be a stalwart bastion of traditionalism—a powerful foe of that change it does not understand, which seems threatening to its status, or in which it does not participate. Furthermore, as the origin and conditioner of many top executives and elder statesmen, the strong ties of respect, loyalty, and friendship existing among these field-mates may dominate perception and decision-making to the overall detriment of the organization at large.

During the short period of his association with the organization, news of the chief planner's function and person has spread throughout, by a few formal communiques and through intensive use of "the grapevine." Based upon reports now filtering back from various points in "the field," the lower the echelon and the further geographically, the more fragmentation and the higher distortion. Some rumors have reached the point of fantasy. Curiosity is turning to skepticism and, in many cases, anxiety.

In short, "the field" is a culturally separate and operationally indispensable body with which company-wide planning in general, and the chief planner in particular, must be allied in order to survive, function effectively, and prosper.

Immediately following approval of the pre-cycle program and formation of the Corporate Planning Committee, sufficient momentum has been developed to enable headquarters to progress in company-wide planning during a brief absence by the chief planner. It is strongly urged that he now avail himself of the opportunity to visit the field as soon as possible,

- to correct *misconceptions* regarding company-wide planning in general, and himself in particular
- to increase *comprehension* regarding the intent and operations of company-wide planning
- to acquire a better *appreciation* of "the field" as a milieu and contributor
- to commence establishing *rapport* facilitating the interrelations between field operations and company-wide planning
- to create an *image* useful to the planning function in general, and himself in particular
- to site potential *test areas* for planners' field activities
- to determine appropriate *training environs* for field orientation of planners

- to *scout* possible recruits for company-wide planning from the field

The visit should be carefully designed and structured toward these ends. With guidance from the chief executive and Corporate Planning Committee, topics of query should be designated beforehand, locales chosen with a rationale, and key interviewees scheduled in advance. For thoroughness, clarity, and uniformity, the chief planner might prepare a short presentation on his mission as well as methods to be given for introduction at each visited field location. Though received cordially everywhere, the chief planner should assume nothing. He can be certain that extensive evaluations, both officially sanctioned and not, will be made of him and transmitted throughout the organization, for better or for worse.

## § 12.4  GROWTH OF ANXIETY AND RESENTMENT

Shortly after his return from "the field," the chief planner should not be surprised if anxiety and resentment have grown throughout the organization to a level (1) discernible during his interactions with members at all echelons, and (2) detrimental to development of company-wide planning in general. Of the many reasons for this response, five are paramount:

- recognition that the changes possible through company-wide planning are fundamental
- realization that change precipitated by company-wide planning has personal ramifications
- unduly rapid progress of the planning function

- lack of traditional apprenticeship by the chief planner
- refusal of the chief planner to join political cliques

Through mutual orientation, and via the interaction required by joint tasks, increased comprehension of the concepts, philosophies, and techniques of company-wide planning will have occurred throughout the organization. It will be recognized that fundamental changes are indeed possible through company-wide planning, and that they are so far-reaching as to affect the very *raison d'etre* of the organization, its mode of management, and the capacities required within this new milieu for survival and advancement. However, this glimmer of understanding should be tempered by the old adage, "A little knowledge is a dangerous thing." Expectations will be exaggerated as to magnitude and speed of transformation. Those in power may be alarmed, and dissidents heartened.

In an abstract and general context, "greater rationality, system, and consistency" to facilitate "more effective deployment of resources and their management" appears universally and indisputably desirable. With this anticipation of accelerated change comes the realization that it has personal ramifications. Speculation is rampant:

"What will happen to *my* Division? Will *our* Group remain intact? If reapportionment and reassignment of responsibilities occur, where will *I* be? Is *my* status to suffer? Am *I* still in line for that promotion? I've been working so hard to get *my* organization functioning to do the routine. Now that *I* can take it a little easy and do some creative thinking . . .Are they really going to make *me* give up Joe to the Corporate Planning Department?"

Soon, as the chief planner solidifies his political position and builds the Corporate Planning Department, the organization will respond to specific events:

"Hobnobbing with topmost management, getting his program through fast—with a big budget—and staffing up with lots of new recruits as well as some of *our* best men. Isn't this moving too fast for any operation?

"Who is this guy anyway? Came out of nowhere. I wonder how *they* got him. Who does he know? Any connection with big stockholders? No experience in our company. Lots of theory. Spent most of his life thinking, not doing. Hear he's published some stuff. Supposed to be impressive. Looks impressive, uses the right words, speaks well, and does fine presentations. Little doubt that he's competent."

"No one really knows him. Been here too short a time. Works an awful lot, not only during normal hours, but at night and on weekends. What makes him tick? What does he want? What is his real game? Is he shooting for President?"

"Got to give him credit for getting things done, well and fast. But it isn't going to be at my expense. From now on, I'm going to watch this guy like a hawk."

## §12.5 "THE PRESIDENT WISHES TO SEE YOU . . ."

Under certain circumstances, not too hard to imagine, some of these could even be the thoughts of the chief planner's boss, the chief executive. In fact, it is not at all unlikely that if he has made significant headway, the new chief planner will be shortly invited to visit the President regarding the status of his function:

"When we first met, I told you of my impatience to install good company-wide planning. I saw the need and advantages then. You have made us even more aware and eager.

"First, I want to congratulate you on the rapid progress company-wide planning has made in the short time since your arrival. You've impressed us all with your ability to conceptualize the planning process and adapt it to our circumstances. Also, you've done a remarkable job recruiting outstanding staff in this very tight labor market. However, there are some other factors I'd like to discuss so that you may be even more effective in this organization.

"You've disturbed our sales force and offended their Grand Old Man. As you know, he built that organization before becoming President. Even though I have replaced him as chief executive, he can't quite bring himself to retire, and spends a few hours weekly in the office. And he is a Director. While his influence has greatly diminished, he does have a network of friends throughout the company. Even though fairly inactive, he gets on my back when annoyed. You and I agree that our entire marketing function needs an overhauling, and that speed is crucial. But would you try to go a little bit easier on them?

"The Personnel Department is perturbed. They don't understand why you can't staff from candidates within the organization. This is especially so regarding secretaries. I know that you have been reasonable and precise in your specifications, and that we have approved them. I recognize with you that certain skills are required that we haven't developed internally, and that Personnel has not been successful in securing appropriate incumbents from outside. I also realize that implementation of your program in quality and on time depends upon availability of these capacities. To smooth things over, couldn't you bend a little bit?

"Another thing. Some of the boys are irritated by what they feel is your apparent criticism of their pace and working hours. Further, I am told that your evening and weekend sessions are not welcomed, and that they don't feel compelled to attend. I am aware that you've scheduled these sessions to accommodate those who say their daily routines do not permit participation during ordinary working hours. You know that I will work with you at any time. But would it be possible to observe our normal schedule?

"Also, you've rubbed Data Processing the wrong way. They feel that your requests for data in nonstandard forms and with rapid service are unreasonable. You know that they have done the best job in the industry supporting our sales force, and that customer service has come first with us. While it would be nice if scientific work, such as yours, could be expected at the drop of a hat, programmers are awfully hard to get. Can you hold off on these demands?

"In this vein, the Controller feels put out by your insistence that budgeting, programming, and planning, be consistent. Well, right now that is. He's in the middle of a system change-over and a special analysis for . . ."

# CHAPTER 13

# *Inclusion of Middle Management*

> *The only thing we have to fear is fear itself.*
> —Franklin Delano Roosevelt

## §13.1 PARTICIPATION

With approval of the pre-cycle program, commencement of its implementation, and formation of the Corporate Planning Committee, the entire organization mounts interest in and knowledge of the concepts, philosophies, and techniques of company-wide planning and concern over their ramifications. Despite its cautious initial exposure to middle management, and subsequent measures to keep this echelon suitably informed, the attitude in this group may have metamorphosed beyond idle curiosity and detached skepticism to inhibiting anxiety in some cases, destructive resentment in others.

This first extension of company-wide planning, and the reaction to it, were the subjects of Chapter 12.

Also, the Corporate Planning Committee, in reviewing the pre-cycle program, and in executing its guidance and support roles, has raised searching questions on a wide range of topics, most of which require intensive contributions from all sectors and levels of the organization.

Therefore, at this point, participation by middle management is highly desirable, and should be encouraged through several committees composed of personnel and Corporate Planning Department staff. These middle management committees, subordinate in scope and stature to, but interlocking with, the Corporate Planning Committee, provide, in their respective bailiwicks

- *guidance* for company-wide planning in general
- *support* for the Corporate Planning Department in particular
- *communication* for mitigation of anxiety
- *debate* for dispersal of resentment

In support of company-wide planning, each committee member would be expected to include entrees to relevant groups, and resources from his own organization unit.

Every middle management planning committee operates in its own echelon and sector to orient and educate in parallel with the Corporate Planning Committee, and with analogous size and member requisites, except that

- each is chaired by the Corporate Planning Department specialist most closely associated with its topic orientation, and

■ the chief planner functions in each, replacing the chief executive as senior member

The efforts of these committees should yield recommendations for refinement of two types, *substance* and *technique*. Substantive matters are channeled through the originating chairman to responsible operating chiefs, and technical issues to appropriate staff personnel. It is emphasized that these committees in themselves have no formal authority. However, from a de facto viewpoint, their influence can be important.

The first task of each committee would be examination of the prior simulation by topmost management, discussed in § 11.2, to review (1) the substance arising from that simulation, and (2) its application in the pre-cycle program. To expedite implementation of the pre-cycle program, refinements in technique, unless crucial, should be deferred in favor of improvements in substance currently significant and readily applied.

To facilitate coordination of efforts, the delineation of these middle management planning committees may be aligned with whatever primary division of labor has been adopted within the Corporate Planning Department. For illustrative purposes, the third stage organization for the Department, outlined in § 3.6 is assumed. A concomitant set of committees would be formed as follows:

■ Strategic Planning Committee
■ Operations Planning Committee
■ Project Planning Committee

The following three sections pursue this illustrative delineation, each describing the possible activities for one of these committees.

## § 13.2 THE STRATEGIC PLANNING COMMITTEE

As illustratively described in § 3.6, the strategic planning subfunction broadly specifies, on a recurrent basis, preferred means of achieving companywide objectives, and is oriented toward deployment of resources, through

- derivation of overview intelligence
- establishment of parameters for objectives, and standard values for them
- identification of resources and their allocability
- formulation of policies to achieve objectives within constraints

Observing size and membership requisites analogous for its echelon and sector to those described in § 12.1, within context of the role described above, an illustrative roster could be

- Director of Strategic Planning, chairman
- chief planner, senior member
- Director of Marketing Research, member
- Director of Research and Development, member
- Chief Legal Counsel, member
- Planning Administrator, secretary

In its first task—examination of the prior simulation by topmost management—the primary critique would concentrate upon

- *preferences* of claimants upon the organization
- *feasibilities* afforded by the external environment

- *attributes and deficiencies* of the organization, in these contexts

As a result of this activity, the committee would derive a cascade of further queries and recommendations focusing on the *consistency* of

- objectives, constraints, and resources
- missions, and, policies

During the pre-cycle program, this critique would have impact in

- a review of relevant *technologies* for establishing feasibilities
- development of *passive expectations* for the relevant industry(ies)
- generation of *industry standards* from the foregoing

Subsequent to the pre-cycle program, these three activities would be emended and refined with each planning cycle, augmented with timely emphases upon

- *strategies* of all types
- *diversification estimates*, including new processes, products, markets, and locales, as defined in § 3.2 and § 12.2
- specifications for *acquisitions* of the foregoing, including purchase of companies possessing desired capacities
- specifications for *divestments* of the foregoing, including sale of present organization units

## §13.3  THE OPERATIONS PLANNING COMMITTEE

As illustratively described in §3.6, the operations planning subfunction narrowly specifies, on a recurrent basis, preferred means of implementing strategic plans, and is oriented toward management of resources once they have been strategically deployed, through

- derivation of detail intelligence concerning the immediate environment
- establishment of subparameters for goals, and standard values for them
- delineation of operations constraints within the context of mission
- development of systems for managing deployed resources
- formulation of procedures to achieve goals within given constraints through the foregoing system

Observing size and membership requirements appropriate for its echelon, sector, and role, an illustrative roster could be

- Director of Operations Planning, chairman
- chief planner, senior member
- Controller, member
- Director of Data Processing, member
- Director of Sales Management, member
- Planning Administrator, secretary

In its initial assignment, examination of the prior simulation by topmost management, concentration would be on

- criteria for *design* of the company-wide planning system
- *feasibilities* afforded by the actual planning system now in use
- *attributes and deficiencies* of the organization, in these contexts

Based upon this critique, the Committee would produce a group of additional queries and recommendations concerned with the *consistency* of

- determination of *data* types, qualities, and frequencies, for company-wide planning
- *format* for collection and presentation of the foregoing

During the pre-cycle program, the Committee's critique would affect

- development of currently workable *data processing methods* from the de facto system
- flow charting and scheduling generation of passive, expansion, and diversification *expectations* for the organization, as defined in § 3.2 and § 12.2
- specification for short range *performance standards* for the organization

Subsequent to the pre-cycle program, its previously cited activities would also be emended and refined with each planning cycle, augmented with timely emphases upon

- *operations* of all types
- *passive estimates*, including current and incipient

processes, products, markets, and locales, as defined in § 3.2 and § 12.2
- development of *systems* for planning and control
- applications of *management science* and *industrial engineering* to the foregoing

## § 13.4   THE PROJECT PLANNING COMMITTEE

As previously described in § 3.6, the project planning subfunction conducts research and analyses, on a non-recurrent basis, regarding the

- effect of internal environment upon feasibility of organization objectives, the process of planning for their achievement, and the rate of change most appropriate
- simulation of the probable impact from new processes, products, markets, and locales, upon organization performance
- solidifying preliminary plans for new processes, products, markets, and locales, to fill the gap between operations expectations and organization objectives

Again adapting its size and membership for echelon, sector, and role, an illustrative roster could be

- Director of Project Planning, chairman
- chief planner, senior member
- Treasurer, member
- Director of Personnel, member
- Director of Product Planning, member
- Planning Administrator, secretary

This Committee's lead-off project, examination of the prior simulation by topmost management, is addressed to

- *feasibilities* afforded by the internal environment
- identification of *incipient* processes, products, markets, and locales
- *attributes and deficiencies* of the organization, in these contexts

This project would generate further queries and recommendations regarding the *consistency* of

- the quality and quantity of the organization's *manpower*
- the extent of both underemployment and, unemployment of *resources*

During the pre-cycle program, this critique would influence

- appraisal of *flexibility* in resource reallocation
- generation of a crash program for *training* personnel in company-wide planning
- development of realistic *goals* for the major organization units

Subsequent to the pre-cycle program, the above activities would be emended and refined with each planning cycle, augmented with timely emphases upon

- nonrecurrent *projects* of all types
- *expansion estimates,* including related processes, products, markets, and locales, as has been defined in § 3.2 and § 12.2

- development of *techniques* on one-of-a-kind basis, for management estimates, including forecasting
- search for and evaluation of *acquisitions and divestments* in accord with specifications from the strategic planning subfunction

## §13.5   CONTRIBUTIONS AND CATHARSIS

At this point, it will be useful to recall that the middle management planning committees were formed to provide

- guidance for company-wide planning in general
- support for the Corporate Planning Department in particular.
- communication for mitigation of anxiety, and
- debate for dispersal of resentment.

In short, these organization units are designed as vehicles for middle management contribution to and catharsis regarding company-wide planning.

The middle management planning committees are subordinate to but interlock with the Corporate Planning Committee, since members hold appointments in several, and the chief planner is included in all. Thus, continuity, consistency, and efficiency are facilitated through this control on the possibility of gaps, conflicts, and overlaps between committees.

As noted earlier, the committees draw their support from members' organization units, including the Corporate Planning Department, and that resultant recommendations are channeled through the appropriate chairman to responsible operations or staff chief. While these committees do not possess formal authority, their de facto influence can be important.

The work of the committees will often be interdependent. Comparison of the illustrative committees and their suggested activities, in § 13.2 through § 13.4, reveals an implicit division of labor along two axes, (1) substance, and (2) time horizon. In the example offered, the Strategic Planning Committee generally deals with the greatest substance and longest time horizon, the Project Planning Committee is intermediate, and the Operations Planning Committee is procedurally oriented to the short range.

The advantages and disadvantages of committees have been thoroughly discussed in management literature. Their recommended use here recognizes that costs of anticipated benefits should be weighed. Utilized appropriately, this committee scheme offers a balanced path to middle management contribution and catharsis in both the pre-cycle program, and thereafter.

*Part Four*

# THE SYSTEM
# IN
# OPERATION

# CHAPTER 14

# Starting
# the Planning Cycle

*A journey of a thousand miles
begins with but a single step.*
—Chinese proverb

## § 14.1 THE INITIATING INSTRUCTIONS

Let us assume that the objectives, constraints, and resources arrived at through simulation by topmost management have been reviewed by the Corporate Planning Committee and middle management planning committees. With guidance and support by these groups, the amended pre-cycle program has been implemented at least in its gross aspects. Through these efforts, an extensive background now exists of descriptions, queries, appraisals, and recommendations on substance and technique, feasibilities and probabilities, the company-wide planning system and its satellites, and data management for the entirety. The organization is now poised for its first company-wide planning cycle.

Each company-wide planning cycle is initiated by a

set of *instructions*, written by the chief planner considering all relevant prior activities, and issued from the chief executive to operations and staff chiefs directly concerned. These instructions, ideally available in booklet form with main body and amplifying appendices, provide *context*, describe *requirements*, and specify *schedule* for the particular company-wide planning cycle in question. Explicitly, the instructions contain a

- statement of *objectives and goals* for the overall organization and each of its major units
- description of primary *assumptions and constraints* to which planning is expected to adhere
- prescription of required *format* for text and data presentation, and a *schedule* for completion of both intermediate and final versions
- review of general *responsibilities* for planning and specific *assignments*

While each element in this information package is vital, the above arrangement is suggestive, and should be adapted to the particular organization and its circumstances. However, the pattern presented here will; be pursued, for illustration, throughout the remainder of the chapter.

## §14.2  OBJECTIVES AND GOALS

The instructions initiating each company-wide planning cycle contain a statement of objectives and goals for the overall organization and each of its major units. Identification of the underlying parameters for measurement and control, and their standard values, are also included. As earlier defined,

- An *objective* is a broad aim or ultimate end toward which a plan is designed and implemented.
- A *goal* is a specified achievement, supporting a superordinate objective, measurable at a scheduled point in time, toward which a program is designed and implemented.

For example, an objective and one of its supporting goals could be "become the leading growth company in the aviation electronic industry, with an average annual increase in per share earnings over the next five years of 20%," and, "design, produce, and market a combination omninavigation and distance-measuring transceiver for private pleasure aircraft, by 1 July, 1971, priced at $500."

The objectives and goals stated at the initiation of each planning cycle result from prior activities. For the first planning cycle, the antecedents are the top management simulation and the committee critiques already discussed.

Confusion and confrontation in the phrasing and use of goals statements will often occur immediately prior to their imminent dissemination before the first planning cycle. The planners will prescribe realistic goals based upon probable circumstances and capacities. For leadership purposes, operations chiefs will often advocate optimistically high and subjectively derived motivational targets. In the name of "conservatism," financial executives will tend to pessimistic performance standards, with associated underemployment of resources.

To promote realism in planning and implementation, it should be made clear that stated goals are not immutable. On the contrary, they are certain to be reviewed as part of the planning process, and with better insights and altered circumstances, analytically support-able changes in goals will, of course, be instituted. In fact, proposals for such modifications—perhaps elimina-tions or unrelated additions—are expected, solicited, and necessary.

Such realistic goals can then be utilized as bases, appropriately translated, in the very legitimate but quite different purposes of internal motivation and external financial community relations.

## § 14.3 ASSUMPTIONS AND CONSTRAINTS

Approved by the chief executive, assumptions and constraints to which planning is expected to adhere during the imminent cycle are also described in the initiating instructions. To reiterate, definitions typing these premises are

- A *value premise* underlies and formulates a pref-erence.
- A *fact premise* is empirically verifiable by obser-vation.
- A *condition* is a premise upon whose fulfillment implementation of a plan or program rests, or the veracity of an estimate is founded.

An example of each is, in order, "sacrifice current income for future capital appreciation," "the service industries have exhibited steadier growth in per share earnings and higher return on capital than manufac-turing, although the latter has afforded higher current income," therefore, "for the purpose of this plan, assume our continued shift to the former." Another condition, a pure constraint, would be "however, contain your plans within the legislative barriers to our further penetration of commercial banking within the U.S."

The primary assumptions and constraints should cover every relevant area as an overall framework within which subordinate premises will be generated and aligned during the planning process, so that the primary premises may themselves be complemented, altered, or even refuted.

Systematic development of comprehensive and consistent primary premises can be aided through the structuring of matrices in which the three row factors would be

- behavioral
- technological, and
- financial

and two column headings might differentiate each of the preceding factors as

- external to the organization, and
- internal, for the organization as a whole

Following this, another matrix could subdivide material for the organization per se internally by

- component organization units, and
- management functions

Other cross-classifications transcending the above-mentioned categories would be

- process
- product
- market
- locale

The *behavioral* premises deal with such aspects as cultural values, social institutions, political power, organization structure, group formation, and personality characteristics. The *technological* is concerned with input, process, and output in physical terms, and the description, efficiency, scale effects, and latitudes of these. And *financial* assumptions pertain to monetary phenomena such as the unit of account, medium of exchange, and store of value, and associated topics, including velocity of circulation, interest rates, and the pricing impacts of these.

*External* premises deal with the host environment— global, regional, national, and industry. *Internal* assumptions (1) pertain to the organization itself in each context, and (2) are further divided to represent each component organization unit alone, and (3) may again be separated by the management functions permeating all organization activities.

Cross-classifications by process, product, market, and locale can further define the preceding categorizations. In lieu of better knowledge, arbitrary suppositions on these matters may be utilized. These suppositions could be especially important where organization units are inextricably interdependent, and imposed uniformity is preferred to anarchic discretion.

Whatever the scheme for primary assumptions and constraints, the categories, and the priorities of one class over the other, should be utilitarian. The totality facilitates company-wide consistency and realism, on the one hand, and affords tangible opportunity, on the other hand, for evolutionary improvement through the planning process itself. Keep in mind that an accepted program from the ongoing planning cycle may influence the primary premises of its successor.

## § 14.4  FORMAT AND SCHEDULING

Given the identification of underlying parameters to be institutionalized by company-wide planning for measurement and control, and their standard values, application requires

- the designation of specific *data* type, quality, and frequency, to represent each parameter
- establishment of protocols for their *approximation* and *calculation,*
- *format* for collection and presentation of the foregoing, and
- development of currently workable *data processing methods*

All of the above are accomplished during the precycle program, at least on a tentative basis, through the efforts of the Operations Planning Committee in our illustration. In consonance, that committee, again in a preliminary manner flow charts and *schedules* generation of passive, expansion, and diversification estimates.

To communicate the conclusions of these deliberations in an immediately useful manner, and induce conformity with them, the instructions initiating each planning cycle should include a section prescribing required *format* for text and data presentation, and a *schedule* for completion of both intermediate and final versions.

The format instructions for text presentation would have a table of contents specifying topic headings, pattern of organization, indexing system, and clerical protocol.

For data presentation, the specifications require utilization of standard forms for data transcription and their subsequent manipulation, procedures for immediate and finished processing, and lists for ultimate distribution. In addition, those situations where graphic depictions are desirable would be indicated, with a uniform layout for display.

The schedule is useful in both flow chart and tabular form. The flow chart shows the designed flow of data during the company-wide planning cycle, between organization units, and along a time scale. This provides a visual impression of the totality. The tabular form demarks, in calendar fashion, the specific contributions required from each organization unit, and their due dates.

The entire format and scheduling effort is intended to make data management for the company-wide planning cycle effective in terms of end use, and yet as unobtrusive as possible to the procedural stability of the organization. The uniformity so engendered in intermediate and final products greatly facilitates verifying, comparability, and aggregation.

The utility of the entire company-wide planning function literally depends upon designation of appropriate data, identification of suitable sources, successful format for collection and presentation, and efficient processing and dissemination. Thus, neither the demands of these tasks nor the benefits from their effective performance should be underestimated.

It was stated in §3.6 that the administrative aspects of company-wide planning—both to the overall function and within the Corporate Planning Department—are likely to be onerous, making highly desirable the establishment of a subgroup expressly for this purpose. Because of the dominance of relations with middle management, supervisory personnel, and clerical elements, inadequate attention to this interface can generate friction, cause great inefficiency, and even paralyze activities on a wide scale. Applying, extending, refining, and enforcing format and scheduling is the *raison d'etre* for the administrative subfunction of the Corporate Planning Department suggested in §3.6. A rereading of that description at this point would be beneficial.

However, whether or not this administrative subfunction within the Corporate Planning Department is in fact recognized as such, and separately organized and staffed, will depend upon the perceptivity of management and the work load undertaken. Unfortunately, to the detriment of company-wide planning, "the squeaking wheel usually gets the oil." It ordinarily requires ulcer-producing frustration, obvious inefficiency, and damning outbursts, before this relatively lowly "addition to overhead" is given reasonable attention and support.

## §14.5  RESPONSIBILITY AND ASSIGNMENT

To facilitate execution of the planning process as intended, the instructions initiating each planning cycle should contain a review of general *responsibilities* for planning and specify *assignments*. For edification of the many individuals involved in company-wide planning, it could commence with a summary of responsibilities for company-wide planning, stressing that the relevant operations chief is responsible for *substance* in his plan, but *technique* is the province of appropriate staff personnel, and continuing with a brief statement of the various key roles, perhaps excerpting from the source job descriptions. In this context, the chief executive is the top arbiter on the substance of plans, and the chief planner on the technique of planning.

In complementary fashion, the purpose, structure, membership, and aid available from each planning committee of Chapters 12 and 13 should be noted.

It warrants reiteration that the Division Planning Function is an inseparable component of the Division Chief's role, operating under technical surveillance of the Corporate Planning Department. As such, the Division Chief has discretion to accommodate the planning function by recourse to his own efforts, by multiple assignments of personnel from within his organization unit, and by aid from the Corporate Planning Department. However implemented, the Division is responsible for furnishing contributions to the company-wide planning function as approved by the chief executive. Such contributions, of course, are expected to adhere to specified format and schedule.

Enforcement of responsibilities in company-wide planning can be bothersome, and even excruciating, especially during the first planning cycle, some major reasons being

- Company-wide planning requires *perspective* of and *deference* to the organization as a whole, rather than to any sub-unit thereof.

- The Corporate Planning Department, as a new organization unit, upsets the *balance of power* and ambient flow of data existing before its establishment.
- The chief planner will likely have precipitated *anxiety and resentment*, as discussed earlier.
- Exercise of *quality control* on the planning process and its output by the Corporate Planning Department.

The last is always particularly troublesome, for it necessarily requires judgement of relative intangibles related to rationality and reliability. Some material rejected on those counts might otherwise have been considered sacred within the realm of company folklore or industry mythology.

Often out of habit, and sometimes in retaliation, operations chiefs will attempt to bypass the Corporate Planning Department in its prescribed sphere of responsibility, ignoring format and schedule instructions, and failing to consider recommended changes in plan. Should the chief executive tolerate this flaunting of organization discipline, he will develop an emasculated planning function, and invite overall anarchy.

# CHAPTER 15

# *Executing the Process of Planning*

*When you can measure what you are speaking about, and express it in numbers, you know something about it.*
—Lord Kelvin

## § 15.1 ESTIMATES AND ANALYSIS

Instructions initiating the planning cycle, written by the chief planner and issued from the chief executive, are disseminated to all operations and staff chiefs directly concerned.

To encourage creative contributions rather than mechanical compliance, it is important to stress by word and demonstrate by deed that

- The relevant operations chiefs are responsible for substance in their plans, but technique is the province of appropriate staff personnel
- Changes will be considered in stated objectives and

goals and described primary assumptions and constraints, when requested with analytical support
during the planning cycle

Upon receipt of the instructions initiating the planning cycle, the first step is derivation of passive expectations, defined in § 3.2:

**passive expectations** estimates of performance and
resources associated with *current and incipient*
processes, products, markets and locales.

To further circumscribe that concept, the definition
of *estimate* is reiterated as a conditional forecast expressed in terms of approved parameters and their
standard values.

So, within the environment, external and internal,
sketched by the instructions, and using the approved
means and form of expression, verbal and quantitative,
each major organization unit derives the set of passive
expectations associated with its responsibilities and assignments. This is done with the cooperation and aid of
other relevant groups, operations and staff, in accord
with the schedule prescribed.

To develop greater reliability in estimates, the deriva-
tions may occur in context of multiple supposed environments, perhaps in one optimistically high, and another
pessimistically low, thereby evolving realistic limits for
credibility and contingency.

In its quality control subfunction, the Corporate
Planning Department adjudges adherence to the instructions, suitability of topic and technique, and rationality
and reliability.

All passive expectations are aggregated by the Corporate Planning Department, which then executes *gap analysis* by matching these with associated objectives, describing disparities as to both magnitude and timing. The magnitude of the gap is multidimensional, measured through each of the parameters in the company-wide planning system. The nature of this gap will be in accord with the parameters by which it is gauged, and the time period in question.

At this juncture, topmost management engages in fundamental deliberations as to the acceptability of performance represented by the passive expectations on the one hand, and the associated objectives on the other hand. In particular, the multidimensional character of the gap will ultimately result in incomparabilities, interdependencies, and circularities in remedy. While expertise in planning should reduce these circumstances to their fundamental issues, and precipitate them for top management consideration at minimal frequency, their final resolution is solely through the perception and creativity of the responsible decision-makers.

Based upon these determinations, and as a foundation for further planning during this cycle, a *revised gap* is described by the Corporate Planning Department, and disseminated to the original recipients of the initiating instructions with approved amendments thereto.

It is suggested that review of the system concept described in § 3.1 and § 3.2 would now be helpful to readers in preparation for the remainder of this chapter.

## § 15.2  MULTIPLE PLANS

In accord with the amended instructions, and within their respective bailiwicks, responsible personnel now refine their passive expectations, if necessary, as a foundation for filling the revised gap. It is recalled that such encompass current and incipient processes, products, markets, and locales. On these bases are generated, as defined in §3.2,

> **expansion expectations** estimates of performance and resources associated with *related* but not incipient processes, products, markets, and locales, and
>
> **diversification expectations** estimates of performance and resources associated with processes, products, markets, and locales *unrelated* with current and incipient activities.

Under appropriate quality control, all estimates are then aggregated, and a gap analysis is again executed by the Corporate Planning Department.

Topmost management deliberates anew upon performance and objectives, from which another revised gap is described by the Corporate Planning Department.

This process is repeated as necessary, in whole or in part, until responsible personnel are satisfied that

1. The assumptions and constraints are *realistic* and applicable.
2. The stated objectives and goals are *achievable* in this context.
3. The formulated expectations are sufficiently *reliable* to act upon.

Each major organization unit then develops overall plans, subordinate programs, and supporting budgets, as defined in § 12.2, to translate their already extensive efforts in these directions into action sequences with controlled acquisition and use of resources.

The scheme of classification, priority, and presentation for these should be commensurate with the current strategy of organization per se. Whether by process, product, locale, and market, or, organization unit, and management function, each version will have explicit or implied, its

- operations plan,
- expansion plan, and
- diversification plan

## § 15.3  MATHEMATICAL METHODS

As used here, the phrase *mathematical methods* encompasses both formal logic and its quantification.

- *logic* deals with the canons and criteria of inference and demonstration.
- *quantification* expresses subject matter in definite amounts.

Phrasing of the former can be verbal; both could be expressed in terms of symbols, and the latter is most usually numerical.

The extraordinary generality, comprehensiveness, and refinement of expression through mathematical methods, and, the unusual degree of insight gained from their use, have obvious utility in the identification, statement, and analysis of business problems—both those perceived to be complex, and others actually found thereby to be so.

For those able to cope with the abstract, mathematical methods, because of their breadth and penetration, can have greatest impact at the substantive level. It is here that complex situations may be unraveled and posed in elemental form, sometimes with pristine clarity, to assist the exercise of managerial prerogative and decision.

However, because of unfamiliarity with and fear of mathematics by the large majority of topmost management, these methods, if used at all, will ordinarily be at the procedural level, employed by technicians on secondary and mundane phenomena. Even here, unusual value can be obtained in situations characterized by complexity and associated with sufficient resources to make rapid and sensitive management reaction tangibly useful.

For planning, mathematical methods have been utilized in the following ways:

- to *conceptualize* fundamental objectives through symbolization
- to *phrase* strategies through formal logic
- to *preselect* alternatives through analysis of magnitudes
- to *estimate* performance through simulation
- to *communicate* data through quantification

This list is not intended to provide a complete enumeration of history or potential.

However, the use of mathematical methods in business planning has been fragmentary and sporadic, especially as ascent occurs in the organization hierarchy. As with any powerful tool, misinterpretation and misuse can engender hostility and rigidity. One trial often results in condemnation of all such methodology, because of ignorance and fear unopposed by champions in topmost management.

There is a common and mistaken notion that mathematical methods and the computer are inextricably coupled. This is by no means necessarily so. Furthermore, it is not unusual to find data processing personnel devoid of knowledge on and even resentful toward mathematical methods, as will be discussed in the following section.

## §15.4 THE COMPUTER

As we use it, the term *computer* is taken to mean stored program electronic digital machinery, with ancillary equipment, and supporting administrative and technical staff. In accord with circumstances, it can do much to aid or hinder effective execution of the planning process.

The computer processes data electronically. The two most popular phrases typifying system design for performance of this function are

- the *management information concept* which offers, on demand, current reports on any quantified aspect of the organization
- the *total system concept* which infers that all managerial data processing is to be by computer

Both are ideals, with the second more visionary than the first. In actuality, application of the computer in management is usually partial, depending upon the very interrelated influences of the

- stage of organization development
- level of managerial sophistication
- condition of the de facto data processing system
- volume, urgency, and complexity of data processing requirements

The cost and benefits of present and potential electronic data processing are seldom fully tangible. The degree of computerization is largely influenced by management judgment and style on the one hand, and salesmanship by the machine suppliers on the other.

Preference for tangible benefits has oriented management use of the computer toward mere emulation of clerical functions, albeit at an electronic pace. The encompassing and advanced information system concept is difficult to implement and seldom seen, not only due to the inherent procedural problems, but also because many data processing supervisors appear incapable of the necessary perspective. This is due in great measure to their middle and lower management accounting backgrounds. The same is true, but to a lesser extent, regarding suppliers' sales and service representatives.

Unfortunately, such data processing personnel, often in combination with suppliers' representatives of similar ilk, stymie more effective management use of the computer. Furthermore, the suggestion of greater progress, or even the presence of knowledgeable professionals elsewhere in the organization, are often taken by such personnel as a threat to be severely dealt with. The extra-ordinary growth of electronic data processing, and the tremendous shortage of barely skilled, not to say qualified, technicians, has made this condition one so general that it is most often tolerated with little recourse.

In order to surmount this typical circumstance wherein management use of the computer is mired in mediocrity, it is useful to differentiate electronic data processing activities into two classes: routine and creative.

The *creative* aspect can be defined to exclude clerical emulations, and to include the programming and running of material associated with the mathematical methods just described. Once this division of labor is acknowledged, the creative type may be performed internally through separate appendages contained within the Corporate Planning Department or externally through consultants, thus simultaneously accomplishing the task and eliminating this persistent deficiency.

The former option, separate facilities within the Department, is usually to be preferred for creative EDP. It can be most easily accomplished by coupling the scientific programming skills of analysts within Corporate Planning, assuredly on a part-time basis, with one of the miniature computers now becoming available. This combination is, overall, inexpensive considering the time lost in central computer scheduling, and surveillance through the other alternatives by which routine and high volume work must still be accomplished.

When a creative program is routinized, it passes to the routine category for inclusion within the de facto data processing system. However, application of such programs, even when "debugged" will still have to be controlled by those who understand their use.

Assuming requisite latitude, management utilization of the computer throughout the organization could include

- recording and filing of data
- performing arithmetic calculations
- solving mathematical equations
- drawing graphs and diagrams
- monitoring established management programs

By decreasing human participation in routine tasks, the computer can significantly enlarge opportunities for creative management. The benefits of such knowledgeable computer technique in the planning function would be that

- data input *scope* is extended
- data *retrieval* is deepened
- development and automation of *decision rules* are facilitated
- decision-making is rendered more *consistent*
- the *impact* of diverse circumstances upon performance may be simulated more reliably prior to actual exposure of resources
- gaps and/or overlaps in strategies and tactics can be more completely exposed through *simulation* prior to actual application

In agreement with the adage "garbage in garbage out," it is emphasized that there is no such thing as *management by computer* per se. Rather, routinization, by mathematical methods, can be carried forth in a surprisingly effective manner often displacing what was previously considered, due to impaired perception, as judgemental or creative. This has been widely accepted in clerical applications, and can be so in other areas of management as well. It was suggested that the Corporate Planning Department start early in this direction with the employment of its second and third professionals as illustrated in stage two, § 3.6.

However, this enthusiasm for creative utilization of the computer in management should not be misconstrued. The primary contribution of planning is conceptual, and its greatest impact is with substance, not procedure. To the extent that the computer can aid in this orientation, it will then be a powerful tool, but only a tool.


### § 15.5  CONTROL

In this text, the term *control* is a management function comprised of two continuously applied activities

- *detection* of significant discrepancies between the de facto status on the one hand, and the approved plan, its subordinate programs, and supporting budgets on the other hand
- *correction* of these discrepancies, by changing the de facto status to conform with the approved plan, its subordinate programs, and supporting budgets

Control should be effected for every parameter institutionalized by company-wide planning, at every level in the organization, and in all matters, spanning the inclusive range from substance to procedure. As specifically concerned with company-wide planning, control occurs before, during, and after, the planning cycle.

*Before* the planning cycle, standards for control are circumscribed with the delineation of feasibilities, and, the formulation of preferences. The first affords limits upon activities, de facto and potential, nondiscretionary to the organization. Within context of the first, the second narrows the permissible range of described activities, de facto and potential. The two, when melded and formalized, result in the parameters institutionalized by company-wide planning for measurement and control, and their standard values. It is in terms of these that fundamental objectives are phrased, constraints are defined, and resources identified.

*During* the planning cycle, control commences with the issuance of the instructions initiating the planning cycle. To recall, they state objectives and goals, describe primary assumptions and constraints, prescribe format for text and data presentation, schedule intermediate and final versions, and review relevant responsibilities and assignments. Compliance with these instructions and their amendments made during the planning cycle, is maintained through the Corporate Planning Department at two levels:

- control of *topic and technique*
- control of *format and schedule*

Also *during* the planning cycle, control of substance—always the province of topmost management—is exercised on an intermittent basis through interim gap analyses inherent in the planning process, described earlier.

*After* the planning cycle, control is implemented through the subordinate programs and supporting budgets comprising the overall plan. Definitions of these terms are repeated here for convenient review:

- A program is a set of specified actions, designed to achieve the goals cited therein, and scheduled for execution in the future.

■ A budget is an operations plan expressly for coordination of resource acquisition and use, reflecting the comprehensive plan and particular program supporting it, and generally focusing upon the short range interval.

The program is utilized as a standard to control the actions of management, whereas, the budget serves likewise with respect to resource acquisition and use.

While minor adjustments and modifications can be proposed, approved, and implemented in budgets, programs, and plans between cycles, the major changes to each occur upon *recycling* the planning process. Thus, the following should be clearly understood:

Any *alteration*, no matter how small, in a budget or its associated program, is, in fact, an act of *planning* and not one of control, and as such implicitly changes the superordinate plan already in force.

Thus, control, as envisioned herein, runs the gamut from procedure to substance. Regretfully, voicing the concept is far easier than its implementation. On the procedural level, the possibilities in scope and speed of control through the computer "make the mind boggle," but are seldom fully attempted for management purposes, more often than not for behavioral reasons touched upon in § 15.4. On the substantive level, control is essentially conceptual, with wider latitude and longer time horizons, usually because of difficulties in symbolization and quantification of measurement. In these circumstances, control depends upon a generous ration of those as yet unsubstitutable factors, human perception and creativity.

# CHAPTER 16

# Planning and the Financial Community

*To an intelligent man you repeat things three times—to the rest of humanity, constantly!*
—E. L. Rodriguez

## §16.1 FINANCIAL SERVICES—A GROWTH INDUSTRY

Our concept for the formal role of the chief planner includes his participation in relations with the financial community, as outlined in §3.5. Chapter 5 amplified a capitalist viewpoint for which the financial community is a focus. This chapter is intended to sketch the milieu in which occurs liaison between a company and the financial community. We commence with dimensions of growth characterizing the industry, then focus upon profound changes incipient and expected, describe the status of investment research and the security analysts within, outline the overlap between research and sales, and discuss the actual liaison itself within this context.

The term *financial community* ordinarily encompasses that collectivity of firms and individuals professionally and technically focusing upon the circulation of money, granting of credit, obtaining funds and capital, offering banking facilities, and making investments. However, as used in this book, emphasis is upon that segment of the community most concerned with investment via marketable securities, primarily stocks.

The financial community is itself a growth industry, both on the retail and institutional levels. To suggest the direction and magnitude of growth, crude and tentative predictions indicate that ten years from now it is probable that

- The proportion of *families earning over $10,000* annually will *double* to half the total of all families.
- The number of people over 45, prime customers of *investment services*, will increase by *17 per cent.*
- The volume of *personal saving* could increase to around 6 per cent of disposable income, approximately $50 billion, and *double* that today.
- *Corporate profits* will climb to $120 billion pre-tax and $71 billion post-tax, generating dividends of $32 billion and retained earnings of $39 billion: with depreciation of $66 billion, cash flow after dividends is $105 billion, or about *double* the current level.
- Assuming today's relation between physical plant, internal funds flow, and long-term funds required,

*external sources* will provide $27 billion, again *double* the present figure.

Hard-pressed to keep pace with present demand for its services, the financial community is even less prepared for the future. In terms of management sophistication, it has been one of the most archaic of industries. Traditionalism and family ties were strong influences in maintaining a status quo structure and power elite. Many financial firms are still characterized by amorphous organization and ambiguous concepts of identity, role, and objectives. Often, the highest ranking personnel are preoccupied with personal participation in operations, especially sales, rather than managing the firm itself.

In context of the evolutionary pattern of business as outlined in § 1.2, outsiders are only now, in significant numbers, assuming positions in topmost management. Formal planning is primarily occupied with applications of a rudimentary and mundane sort, focusing upon repetitive operations within the bounds of single management functions, and scarcely daring to participate in multifunction matters of substance. And most progress of the last decade was a passive reflection of the affluent society in which customer interest, capacity, and sophistication, associated with growing wealth, has generated a crushing demand for financial services, literally forcing the financial community into greater effectiveness.

## § 16.2  FINANCIAL SERVICES IN TRANSITION

Thus, the financial community has been awakening to an era of profound change, which, in the last decade, was characterized by several significant factors.

The paucity of new common stock financing has greatly increased the size and importance of markets for *already issued securities*, at the expense of traditional investment banking and its emphasis upon raising new money.

Pooling of savings by small investors, under professional management, has fostered the *growth of institutions* both in relative and absolute terms. The consequent stunning rise of mutual and corporate pension funds has been accompanied by broadened acceptance of equity holdings, the combination largely responsible for an increase of 14 percent annually in professionally managed capital, resulting in about 40 percent of New York Stock Exchange securities today.

In parallel with this movement of capital to institutions has occurred the gradual entry of nonowner professional managers, much younger and with more technical education than their predecessors, and with them gradual change from partnership to corporate organization.

And importantly, this entire phase occurred within the environment of existing legislation and relative regulatory permissiveness. While the impact of this metamorphosis has been manyfold, the new managers brought with them two properties of youth—iconoclasm and alacrity. With these came more penetrating research concerning investments and rapid response in implementation. In combination with the above, greater *concentration* of resources and higher *volatility* in markets have developed.

Within the financial community per se, the industry structure, seemingly immutable for so many years, has begun to shift. The search for safety and expansion, in some instances approaching near panic levels, has been reflected in ungentlemanly invasion of formerly pro-scribed domains. Investment bankers are entering re-search and retailing, while retailers have begun under-writing. Commercial banks provide long-term capital through loans and private placements. Banks have also increased their efforts in investment counsel and even merger/acquisition work. Security analysts often function as management consultants. Mutual fund firms sell life insurance, insurance companies provide variable annuities, and banks offer vehicles similar to both.

While it is difficult to make accurate predictions of the future status of an industry undergoing such radical change, a few reasonable prognostications can be made.

Rapid growth of institutions will continue to the point where the pressures of large size can significantly erode internal efficiency and external performance. A solution may be greater managerial decentralization, and, eventual divestment of self-contained units. Both result in de facto *proliferation of entities.*

The economics of increasing scale also impacts upon the size of securities blocks traded, which have grown and will continue to grow both in absolute terms and relative to their share of total market. This in turn has caused *bypass of the traditional stock exchanges* through third and fourth markets via nonexchange intermediaries and directly between institutional sellers and buyers.

Greater emphasis upon portfolio performance, due to pressures from more sophisticated investors, will accen-tuate concentration of resources and volatility of mark-ets. This could result in higher portfolio turnover and could invite more expansive and severe *governmental regulation* particularly concerned with (1) preservation of reasonable market stability, and, (2) maintenance of just sales commissions and management fees.

To defend current status and to participate in the expansion and diversification which has already commenced to characterize the industry, acquisitions will continue among like entities, and mergers will occur between complementary units. For example, nationwide wirehouses will buy regional retail operations, and, insurance companies will join with mutual fund managements. The former typifies the search for efficiency in larger scale organization to accommodate an increasing volume of administration. In pursuit of a "full service" concept, exemplified in the latter, the size of parent companies will mount, and with their broadened span of activities, *concentration of power* will increase.

All of these trends point conclusively to an ultimate imperative which is by far more certain than the eventuation of any one of the foregoing predictions alone, and it is that business management in the financial community must rapidly become more competent, aggressive, and professional, if the industry is to sustain its prominent and effective role in the national economy, and if current member firms are to maintain their status.

In summary, the winds of change blowing through the financial community have grown from gentle breezes to gale force.

## § 16.3   INVESTMENT RESEARCH AND SECURITY ANALYSTS

A company's effective representation to the financial community pivots upon response of the investment research function and the security analysts within it. In § 9.1, an investment was defined as the present commitment of resources in anticipation of future benefits therefrom. In general, research is investigation aimed at the discovery and interpretation of facts, including the phrasing and revision of theories or laws and their applications. Thus, when focusing upon the securities of publicly owned U.S. corporations, the purposes of investment research are twofold:

- collection, integration, and presentation of facts regarding the security under scrutiny, and
- evaluation of that security for the specific purpose being considered

To perform this task, the investment research function considers factors such as

- the international political and economic situation
- impact of government policies, especially monetary and fiscal
- expectations for relevant industries
- evaluation of the subject company in general
- capacity of the subject company regarding this particular issue
- image of the subject management in the financial community

The coalescence of influences upon security prices was schematically shown in Figure 5A.

Investment research groups vary in mission, size, and structure. However, responsibilities are usually divided first by separation of equities and fixed income analysis, and secondly, along industry lines. A third, but weak, cross-categorization is by economic function such as durables, intermediary products, nondurables, and services. Another differentiation could be in terms of economic behavior, that is, cyclical, noncyclical, independent growth, and so forth. Whatever rationales are employed, the structure of investment research groups will often be diffused and frequently amorphous for many reasons, some of which are:

- Professional *business management* in the financial community is wanting, and with it, formal planning and control, which, of course, requires parallel organization.
- *Customer inquiries* span the gamut of business and economics, whereas the investment research department is of finite and usually modest dimensions, thereby inviting a wide range of assignments to analysts.
- Because of tremendous growth in the financial community itself, the *supply of analysts* is insufficient, pirating between firms is ordinary, and personnel turnover is high, all leading to multiple assignments as a stop-gap measure.
- Because investment research is still performed as a *craft*, development of analysts is by apprenticeship and prima donnas abound, wreaking havoc with formal organization structure.

Because of the loose form of organization typical in investment research units, analysts are easily and directly accessible. And given the intuitive nature of performance standards for reward and punishment, the analyst is always eager for insights which may enhance his score.

The analyst may be the product of almost any type of formal education. A highly sought combination would be a technical baccalaureate crowned with a graduate degree in business administration. It is only recently that standards for academic knowledge and working experience have been established for certification of financial analysts. The profession is coming of age.

As personal traits, the competent analyst demonstrates an innate ability for translating concepts to quantitative form and back again. He is disciplined in and attuned to hard work including routine drudgery. And certainly, he should develop and maintain the independent viewpoint which makes the difference between mediocrity and success.

This last attribute implies integrity to withstand, from time to time, considerable pressures of great monetary magnitude. And it should be remembered that in the financial community, a man's word is his bond. One breach, and excommunication for life is likely. This is why the overwhelming majority of contracts are initially oral, either by telephone or in person.

## § 16.4  INVESTMENT RESEARCH OR SALES PROMOTION?

Investment research is done by anyone who invests, even if this resource is implicit, casual, and haphazard. However, professional investment research is a business in itself, performed for financial remuneration by such closely allied entities as

- advisory services
- banks
- brokers
- insurance companies
- investment counselors
- management consultants
- mutual fund managements

When offered for use outside their own organizations, payments for such research is by commissions for brokers, subscriptions for advisory services, and fees for the rest, either on a continuous basis as for investment counselors, or on a project basis in the case of management consultants. Any of the above sources may also engage in implicitly rewarded research, available only internally for the firm's own use.

When received by institutions, investment research is usually screened and used by professionals, who possess realistic expectations. Professionals worthy of the name understand the processes by which estimates and opinions are derived, the strengths and weaknesses of the supplier—both the originating firm and authoring analyst. According to circumstances, this externally acquired research may be employed as a primary input or as a check upon work done elsewhere and inhouse. Evaluation of this material is based upon its degree of veracity, preemptive timeliness, and quality of presentation. The consequence of this evaluation, good or bad, is more or less future business for those purveyors.

However, when received by the nonprofessional individual investor, the screening, application, and evaluation of investment research is likely to be amateurish at best, typically inconsistent and emotional, and accompanied by unrealistic expectations. The retail customer has little technical comprehension of the process and limits of investment research, and only the vaguest notion of relative quality from different suppliers. The authoring analyst is almost always a faceless name, and often an anonymous shadow. This client ultimately judges financial service as a totality by the one standard of "Did I make money?" without assaying the multiple and intricate whys and wherefores of which investment research is only a part.

Thus, it is easy to understand that there are two major levels of substance and distribution in investment research—institutional and retail. *Institutional research*, oriented toward the professional, is comprehensive, and supported by extensive backup material, with the authoring analyst available for query on specifics. On the other hand, *retail research*, oriented toward the consumer, is brief and unsupported by backup material and query privileges. Naturally, there is often an overlap where sophisticated individuals utilize institutional research, and, the retail customer receives indirectly the benefits of institutional quality analysis upon which his summary is based.

Except for a few institutional suppliers, investment researchers assume that their customer, the portfolio manager, has specific objectives, defined constraints, decision-making policies, and an investment strategy. Furthermore, it is also implied that an explicit allocation of resources has been made between those destined for marketable securities, and others such as real estate, precious metals and stones, and objets d'art. Analysts focus on individual securities, and leave their combination in portfolio form to the client. However, these presumptions give rise to an extremely significant question:

Can an analyst, in good conscience, provide competent evaluation of a specific security without framing this advice in context of the peculiarities surrounding the individual customer?

To adequately utilize the output of a security analyst, either (1) his representative, the salesman, should be completely familiar with the customer's situation and be able to interpret it, or (2) the customer, himself, must translate his own situation to accommodate the analyst's presentation and evaluate its suitability.

In both cases, the specific security and its prospective owner must be matched, not only as to characteristics, but also in timing. This dictates purchase if suitable, and sale if not. The first includes retention if already owned, and the second, aversion if not.

In the financial community, how much explicitly negative advice is published on securities? Can analysts risk sealing their entrees to companies which may in the future present opportunities for them and their firms in the many facets of financial services, such as investment banking, merger/acquisition, pension fund management, and secondary offerings? In all fairness, there are several ways of indicating negative opinions, one being to offer a "better alternative" and to do so in oral communication, either in person or by telephone. Again, as stressed at the end of § 16.3, in the financial community, a man's word is his bond, and it must be used judiciously.

How is a purveyor of investment research rewarded and punished? Can conflicts of interest among him, his sales representative, and the customer be resolved? Upon these considerations turns the question to which this section is addressed, namely, is it investment research or sales promotion? Real problems could exist, not so much at the institutional level where relations are continuous and the stakes are high, but more so on the retail level where salesmen are difficult to control and customers are relatively unsophisticated and individually less significant.

## § 16.5    LIAISON WITH THE FINANCIAL COMMUNITY

Why should all companies be interested in effective liaison with the financial community? Because the financial community circulates money, grants credit, obtains funds and capital, offers banking facilities, and makes investments. What company can avoid engaging in and being appraised through financial markets? It was contended, in § 5.1, that over a reasonable period of time, the financial community's evaluation of a business is the most encompassing available.

Why should a publicly owned U.S. corporation be especially concerned? It was concluded in § 5.1 that for such a company the most comprehensive single indicator of expected business success is the ratio of common stock price to per share earnings, termed the price-earnings multiple.

In what ways are well-regarded securities desirable for a publicly owned company? It was stated in § 5.5 that attractive securities (1) greatly magnify the firm's resource base, in value and form, for external growth through acquisition, (2) generally benefit all classes of owners, and (3) aid founding entrepreneurs in simultaneously relinquishing control and gaining reward through their sale. In this context, new money is obtained on more favorable terms and secondary offerings can occur at premium prices.

For companies wishing enhancement of their relations with the financial community, and this is particularly so for small or growing or changing companies, it is necessary to establish and maintain effective *liaison with the financial community* in which strategy and implementation of communications are integral to company-wide planning.

This requires (1) that progress information be kept current in support of the company-wide plan, (2) consistency in presentation on these data to the many and varied targets in the financial community, and thus (3) a central point within the company from which such communication emanates and to which inquiries are channelled, even when external counsel is utilized in advisory or intermediary capacity.

A company's effective representation to the financial community requires at least a gross understanding of how that community is structured and operates. Nuances such as group composition and stratification, ethnic affinities, and family interconnections, can be important for relations within this tradition-oriented and somewhat inbred subculture. This is so not only for selecting and dealing with appropriate firms *per se*, but also their clientele as well.

Since effective representation to the financial community pivots upon response of the investment research function and the security analysts within it, knowledge of the function, its organization and orientation in suitable firms, and the relevant analysts, is highly desirable. In particular, once key analysts have been identified, their qualifications, status, and aspirations should be studied as background for determination of best approach to them.

In § 16.4, it was concluded that the specific security and its prospective owners must be matched, not only as to circumstances, but also in timing. The information system of the financial community can be aided immeasurably through the availability of company data compatible with these requirements disseminated in a manner aligned with the structure and mores of that industry. In this context, a company could publish a well enunciated *basic document*, often called a "fact book," which would include

- statement of the firm's objectives, missions, strategies, policies, and resources
- historic analysis of relations between the economy, relevant industries, competition, and the firm's performance
- description of the firm itself, including processes, products, markets, and locales
- depiction of organization structure, and specification of key personnel, including the functioning of company-wide planning
- brief statement of the company-wide plan, including its fundamental parameters, constraints, and standards for performance
- identification of probable difficulties and risks envisioned for execution of this plan

The depth and detail of this basic document would be determined by (1) the degree of foundation data and analysis available within the company, (2) the danger of exposing potentially damaging material by publication, and (3) expected receptivity within the financial community, including the quality and quantity of analyst interest. It is important to note that the company's annual report, usually serving a very different purpose, is inappropriate here and will not ordinarily suffice.

This basic document should be revised annually, with brief progress reports when significant interim events occur. Truthful portrayal and interpretation of both positive and negative aspects will increase credibility to the ultimate benefit of all concerned.

The basic document and its successor interim reports are easily aligned with output readily available from the type of virile company-wide planning function which is the focus of this book. With this in view, the chief planner's role, as described in § 3.5, specifies his participation in relations with the financial community in general, and in collaboration with other responsible persons:

- to develop, interpret, and communicate with the financial community *analyses* relevant to the company
- to perform *liaison* with relevant personnel within and external to the company, in which comprehensive knowledge of these areas is desirable

It was noted that the chief planner complements rather than supplants the Controller, Treasurer, Financial Vice President, and Director of Public Relations in their respective contributions to financial community relations.

Because investment operations rely upon predictions which are subject to uncertainties inherent in considerations of the future, analysts seek personal interchange with the management of firms under scrutiny (1) to confirm or deny conclusions previously reached via their research, (2) to obtain answers to questions unresolved by company information, (3) to appraise the caliber of management via this interaction, and (4) to better judge reliability through the subtleties of that experience.

Therefore, to establish and maintain effective financial community relations, topmost management must occasionally expose itself personally to the private probes of analysts singly, and to public inquisition before analyst groups. These trials should be augmented by visits to key financial firms, just as analysts will more often journey to the headquarters and plant sites of the company.

This communication program, carrying well prepared and succinct messages, (1) will capture the attention of harried analysts, and (2) aid their research output through the convenience of its predigestive format and content. Naturally, such communication should observe the letter and spirit of governmental regulations regarding the dissemination and use of information in the securities business.

This communication should have a definite impact upon security prices. As mentioned in § 9.2, exposure to uncertainty requires commensurate compensation in total yield. In terms of the present value idea discussed in § 9.4, all other things remaining the same, for a given amount of future benefits, as yield rate decreases present value increases. In other words, decreased uncertainty should increase appraisal of any good business situation, and with it, the relative attractiveness of securities representing claims thereon. Translating this, effective representation in the financial community can decrease uncertainty and thereby increase the value of relevant securities in relation to others in the market.

In summary, the financial community—itself a growth industry in transition—is complex and changing. A company's effective representation to the financial community pivots upon response of the investment research function and the relevant security analysts within it. Veracity, timeliness, and presentation of investment research will promote successful matching of a publicly owned company's securities with prospective owners. This is facilitated by liaison with the financial community wherein strategy and implementation of communications are integral to company-wide planning. This requires a central point in the organization capable of furnishing current information in support of the company-wide plan, and its consistent presentation. Basic documents and interim reports, oriented to suitable firms and relevant analysts, are complemented by occasional personal interchanges between topmost management and key financial firms. This should capture analysts' attention and interest, thereby reducing uncertainty and increasing the value of relevant securities in relation to others in the market.

Liaison with the financial community is too important to ignore. It has too much potential to limit it to quarterly summaries of balance sheets and income statements read over the telephone by a laconic controller. This communication is too delicate to allow as a haphazard, unchanneled "happening," dabbled in by a profusion of analysts' buddies within the company. The role is too complex to entrust to a backslapping martini pusher or a dapper lackey conditioned to touting for story space in second-rate publications. And the subsequent impacts are too profound and lasting to be the province of one wind-bag Director who often has lunch with allegedly influential chums on Wall Street.

While consultants may be helpful in an advisory or intermediary capacity, liaison with the financial community should be a concern of topmost management, supporting the company-wide plan, and programmed accordingly.

In today's financial community, the "old school tie"

may help gain a foot in the door, but *performance is what counts* for everyone—the endorsing analyst, prospecting salesman, portfolio manager, and ultimate customer.

*Part Five*

# PITFALLS
# AND
# PAYOFFS

# CHAPTER 17

# Personnel and Politics

> . . . it being my intention to write a thing
> which shall be useful to him who apprehends it,
> it appears to me more appropriate to follow up
> the real truth of a matter than the imagination of it. . . .
> —Niccolo Machiavelli, The Prince

## §17.1  PLANNING BY DIRECTORS AND CONSULTANTS

Can planning be done from outside the organization, say by consultants or perhaps a Director versed in the subject? A simple answer to this simple question is "sometimes." Whether this is the most effective mode depends upon many factors. Some of the more frequent determinants of feasibility are listed in order below:

1. *size* of organization, as measured by number of management personnel
2. *focus* of planning, whether strategy or operations

3. degree and pattern of decision-making *discretion* characterizing the organization
4. *allocability* of resources, in speed and magnitude
5. availability of appropriate *personnel*, internal and external
6. *politics* in decision-making, as it affects preferences and limits alternatives
7. level of management *sophistication*, both current and desired

The *size* of the organization, as measured by the number of management personnel, is a limiting factor on the possibility of implementing a planning process with only intermittent direction from outside the organization and with none from inside. The more management personnel, then the greater intricacy in system design and operations for their participation, and the higher complexity for ingestion of their contributions.

The intended *focus* of planning, whether strategy or operations, determines the degree and frequency of involvement by the organization below its apex. In extreme cases, strategic planning could be performed with data generation and analysis externally, guided by only a handful of topmost managers. Conversely, operations planning requires middle management familiarity with detail and intimacy in implementation.

The degree and pattern of decision-making *discretion* characterizing the organization affects size and focus. If decision-making is highly centralized, then, for a given volume of output, the number of management personnel will likely be less and the focus of planning more ordinary. Thus, for a highly centralized organization, planning may be easier to execute through external aid than otherwise, although this does not imply that such an arrangement will necessarily be most effective.

The *allocability* of resources, amplified in § 8.1, determines the possible pace and magnitude of planning influences. In a situation characterized by administrative rigidity and little decision-making discretion, it is unlikely that a virile and full company-wide planning function could survive. Therefore, to the degree that resource allocability is restrained, the dimensions of company-wide planning are reduced to include operations only, and commensurately, the attractiveness of external execution is increased for the strategic aspects of the function.

The availability of appropriate *personnel* to perform the planning function is an obvious factor in considering the role of external aid. Limitations upon internal supply would be professional competence, political pressure, and personal aspirations. Limitations on the external supply of possible incumbents were posed in § 10.2. With these factors in view, to the degree that candidates are unavailable to staff the planning function, external aid may be the only expedient.

The level of management *sophistication,* current and desired, is perhaps the greatest influence of all upon the choice between external and internal execution of the planning function. A relatively knowledgeable executive corps will already be performing the planning function with some skill, and as a result may realistically perceive both the attributes and deficiencies of more formal, company-wide, and comprehensive planning. The converse is equally true. Therefore, all other things remaining equal, the less adept the organization, the greater is desirability of external aid for company-wide planning.

The *politics* in decision-making, as it affects preferences and limits alternatives, will orient the organization's de facto objectives, constraints, and resources and thereby, its concept of efficiency. The form of planning described throughout this text strives for rationality, system, and consistency. In an environment of intrigue, such a planning function could well be such a common threat to unify all factions just long enough to scuttle it. Should this sort of situation be envisioned, then all but the most rudimentary and mundane operations planning may be done externally, not because this is preferable per se, but rather because it may be the only option open.

From this brief discussion, it should now be apparent that the question of external versus internal planning must be answered within context of the particular characteristics of the organization under consideration, and its circumstances at the time. It is crucial that the type of planning desired be specified. The answer must be a subtle and changing blend of external and internal contributions befitting the specific situation and its evolution.

As a general observation, a plan can be compiled most quickly with extensive external guidance and support. On the other hand, institutionalization of the planning process is a long-term investment in management development which requires a significant internal effort over several years. The mix of planning labor between external and internal sources will be greatly influenced by the trade-off between current desire for a plan *now* as against the conceptualization, installation, and operation of a company-wide planning system in the *future*.

## § 17.2  PERSONNEL SPECIFICATIONS FOR PLANNERS

Another query frequently posed is, "What personnel specifications should guide selection of planners?" The following answer, which may well be arguable, reflects the writer's personal experience. It is assumed that the organization in question has rationally decided to develop the formal, comprehensive, and company-wide planning system described previously, and further, that it is seriously searching for and preparing to effectively host the competent professional planner who will direct its conceptualization, installation, and operation.

It is emphasized that the specifications which follow are for the initial chief planner in the organization's history, that the incumbent will initiate the form of planning described throughout this text, and further, that the circumstances and personalities as discussed in § 3.4, § 3.5, and § 10.1, have been reviewed prior to application of these standards:

### psychological dimensions
- high intelligence
- unusual creativity
- independence of thought
- extraordinary self-discipline

### vocational attributes
- professional orientation
- technical competence
- communications proficiency
- experience in the role

### behavioral characteristics
- perspective in analysis

- tenacity in implementation
- charismatic leadership
- human relations sensitivity

Given the substance and tone of the technical tasks and personal interactions of the initial chief planner, the incumbent should be an applied scientist first, a manager second, and perhaps inclined towards an interest in social anthropology. In addition to these characteristics, the planner must possess insatiable but channeled curiosity, great fortitude, capacity to bear the political risk inherent in innovation, and the personal mobility to exploit opportunities whenever and wherever they arise. Another form of planning and a successor incumbent will perhaps have different qualities. Assuming all the foregoing, an ideal, but not necessary, personal background would be as follows:

- bachelors degree in *applied science* or engineering, with solid evidence of breadth in minor fields and extracurricular activities
- military experience as a junior officer, preferably in *command* positions
- graduate degree in *business* or allied studies such as management, finance, economics, or political science
- *diversified* experience in several industries, organization sizes, and perhaps countries
- *achievement* in a succession of increasingly broader roles concerned with the planning function
- an age range of *thirty-five to forty-five years*, time enough to accumulate this background, youth to bear the political risk inherent in innovation, and

ambition for rewards of the difficult role of initial chief planner

In order of increasing unsuitability, the following are generally *not* appropriate candidates as initial chief planner in the context of this book: pure economists, market researchers, mathematicians and statisticians, accountants, and experts on data processing and computers. All of these skills can be extremely useful in the planning function, and the chief planner should understand and employ them as subordinate aids, but they are each insufficient in themselves.

In accord with intentions for managerial succession, other qualities may be added to those outlined above. This is true not only for the initial chief planner, but also as regards his subordinates, the duties of whom were suggested in the illustrative Corporate Planning Department organizations of § 3.6.

## § 17.3 CONDITIONS OF EMPLOYMENT FOR PLANNERS

A prospective employer is frequently puzzled as to how planners should be treated in terms of supervisory techniques and working conditions. The following observations are offered with the caveat that should precede highly personal opinions on such a subject.

For emphasis let us repeat: the incumbent should be an applied scientist first, a manager second, and perhaps a social anthropologist by avocation. The behavioral implications of these characteristics are significant, especially when contrasted with usual patterns in bureaucracies, whether business or government. Both the planner's values and his means of satisfying them are quite different from those normally encountered, and this must be recognized and accommodated to facilitate effective performance in the Corporate Planning Department.

To furnish broad reference for *reward of planners,* what appear to be prime factors are listed in priority order. While it is most hazardous to generalize, given the heterogeneous character of this new profession and those within it, the risk of being in error is considered preferable to silence:

- tangible *application* of concepts developed and recommendations made
- opportunity to *learn* the organization's functioning in all processes, products, markets, and locales
- achievement of de facto *responsibility and authority* specified in the formal role description
- facility for *professional development* through on-the-job latitude and participation in relevant managerial and academic societies
- commensurate *recognition*, including rank, with inclusion in appropriate governing councils, and parallel remuneration
- freedom from *administrative* involvement, such as dealings in clerical matters, haggling on EDP scheduling, etc.
- flexibility in work day *schedule* and work place *location*, so long as commitments are satisfied for assignments and meetings
- satisfactory *financial compensation* in line with both external standards and internal comparisons

To some, it may be surprising that, in the writer's judgment, *financial compensation* appears relatively unimportant in the planner's scale of rewards. Were that factor of higher priority, the planner would be in another livelihood. His psychological dimensions, vocational attributes, and behavioral characteristics certainly equip him better than most. If material acquisitiveness were more important, such individuals could obviously garner their fair share by any standard. However, the planner, because of his personal orientation, prefers the satisfactions of his profession to activities of a different sort which may be more beneficial financially. Thus, it would be a serious supervisory error to foist upon them an incentive scheme stressing financial remuneration in the same manner as for, say, commission salesmen.

However, it should not be misconstrued that planners are either uninterested in financial compensation or totally altruistic. On the contrary, it is necessary for most of them to support a living standard enjoyed by those of like background. Furthermore, the power of comparison requires remuneration at a level relative to external and internal positions of similar content. Being such a new profession, especially in business, reference must often be to other analogous roles. In this matter, industry could be guided by conditions of employment offered its applied scientists, and the financial community could look to its security analysts.

The chief planner's financial compensation should be aligned with others in his echelon. In business, particularly if an officer, heavy emphasis upon stock options is strongly recommended. Because the role is so difficult to assess in terms of immediately measurable impact, performance can be truly evaluated only in gross as a totality over a significant time period. Stock price tends to reflect company performance in this fashion. Furthermore, who is more concerned with the organization's future than the chief planner?

In view of the personnel specifications for planners suggested in § 17.2 and their allied employment conditions as discussed in this section, some readers not familiar with the values and behavior of applied scientists may now exclaim, "Are these planners *privileged* characters?" Those who understand would reply, "No, not privileged characters—just *different* characters."

Given the breadth of the company-wide planning function, the political instability of its situation, and professional depth of those qualified, it should be apparent that planning is a labor of love to the extent that any paid profession can be.

If the management of planners is pursued along the general guides submitted in this section, the organization will be more likely to attract qualified personnel, retain them once employed, facilitate their typically unusual dedication, and in so doing, benefit by the effective service an appropriately directed Corporate Planning Department can provide.

## § 17.4  SUCCESSION IN THE PLANNING FUNCTION

With evolution of the company-wide planning function in a conventional life cycle pattern, initial emphasis upon conceptualization, strategic innovation, and installation of a basic system gradually gives way to preservation and refinement of these accomplishments, development of satellite planning systems for use in the management functions and operating divisions, and an increasing proportion of project-like efficiency work in management science, operations research, and industrial engineering.

This solidification of the company-wide planning function is likely to be accompanied by the increasing boredom of initial planners due to the mounting procedural nature of their tasks and to parallel escalation of interpersonal abrasion with the organization as the Corporate Planning Department penetrates more deeply and broadly into operations. It is interesting to note that many who have observed this metamorphosis in business enterprises confirm that it takes a rule-of-thumb time span of about *three years*. Also, this period appears to be convenient for major personnel reassignments to and in this function because (1) the career aspirations of incumbents probably now require such turnover, and (2) political expediency will by this time invite it.

This shift from design to operations will occasion the desirability of formally realigning responsibilities throughout the organization vis-a-vis the company-wide planning function. It is likely that the various management functions and operating divisions will have vitally increased their use of sophisticated management technology, and significantly enlarged the resources and personnel devoted to these ends. Thus, the curiosity, skepticism, anxiety, and resentment with which the early Corporate Planning Department was regarded has been transformed to basic comprehension, fundamental respect, grudging tolerance, and even voluntary cooperation.

Accompanying this change may be a de facto demotion of the Corporate Planning Department as its preoccupation with deployment of resources becomes, instead, management of resources already deployed. It was observed in § 3.4 that whether the chief planner should be an officer, and entitled Vice President, depends upon company circumstances. Whatever this decision for the initial chief planner, it should be reviewed in light of new intentions at this juncture. If such a downgrading in departmental stature is in fact contemplated, then perhaps the successor incumbent will enter at a lower rank and wait longer than his predecessor for promotion, if it is at all forthcoming.

Assuming that the organization's experience with company-wide planning—its history and present status, and the organization's intentions for it—is as described in this text, the successor chief planner should be no less intelligent than his predecessor. However, he should more closely identify with the values and behavioral norms of the organization. With greater managerial orientation and political finesse, this individual can be a career employee who has successfully directed associated but narrower functions—such as marketing research or financial analysis, and in this process absorbed sufficient technical knowledge regarding company-wide planning to promise continued achievement in his new role as its leader.

Should this be the course taken, such fundamental changes in the company-wide planning function may well precipitate mass dissatisfaction in and perhaps defection of some Corporate Planning Department subordinates. A few may be retained in that group through rotation of duties. Others could be assigned elsewhere, either in planning-related roles of other management functions or operating divisions, perhaps as directors thereof. .

If the initial chief planner was active in financial community relations, as suggested in §3.5 and §16.5, caution should be taken to prepare relevant security analysts for a shift of personalities in this highly visible function, rather than risk their interpretation of reassignment as indicating basic changes in company objectives, constraints, and resources.

It goes without saying that the initial chief planner is professionally and ethically bound to advise topmost management regarding this natural evolution in his function, and to regulate the pace of transition for the benefit of the entire organization and his departmental subordinates.


## § 17.5 POLITICAL PITFALLS FOR THE PLANNER

As used throughout this book, the term *politics* connotes competition between interest groups or individuals for leadership and power. The very compelling political dimensions of the planning role have been implied sporadically in these chapters. Such phenomena are manifested throughout the organization, in every echelon and sector, especially during initial installation of the company-wide planning function because of its obvious potential as a major force. Some depiction of this situation was attempted in Chapter 12. With the warning that what follows is again "wisdom literature," the purpose of this section is to cite six grievous political pitfalls for the chief planner, all especially meaningful during the initial phase:

1. failure to *specify the role* before employment
2. *forced-draft development* of a company-wide planning system
3. loss of *impartiality and neutrality*
4. *being type-cast* as to capacities and functions
5. *upstaging the chief executive*
6. *undue dedication* in the performance of duties

Failure to specify the role before employment, especially for the initial planner, could be disastrous for the organization as well as the individual. Delineation of this role was the topic of § 10.1 through § 10.3. For the benefit of all concerned, it was advocated that preagreement and documentation be obtained through (1) an appropriate job description, (2) a conceptual framework for the function, (3) a program for its installation, (4) commensurate support through a financial and personnel budget, and (5) an employment contract. Standards are derived from these instruments by which performance of the chief planner and his department is periodically evaluated.

Some might argue that such precise definition beforehand could result in rigidity. On the contrary, this formalism leads to clarity, and only its inept application need result in difficulty.

Forced-draft development of the company-wide planning function occurs either from desire of the chief planner to rapidly demonstrate superior performance, or, by pressure of the chief executive, perhaps for the same reason. Both may exhibit insensitivity to and underestimation of organizational inertia and resistance. It is normal not to fully recognize the fundamental ramifications of company-wide planning in its transformation of the organization's cultural values, social institutions, and the power structure.

For instance, the chief executive may admonish his new planner that "I am an impatient man—I want to see results—and fast." However, if this is taken literally and reflected in an accelerated schedule for system conceptualization, installation, and operation, the chief planner may soon see that his superior shies from inflicting and enduring the pain which in some degree necessarily accompanies change through dissonance and strain.

In observing de facto behavior rather than listening to stirring exhortations, the chief planner should be pleasantly surprised if he does not find that management's trade-offs are weighted in favor of harmony. Thus, persistence in forced-draft development could easily result in suspension of the entire company-wide planning function. As a colleague once remarked, "You can't pistol-whip a bunch of old men and get away with it."

The planner is in a difficult social position within his organization. The role, as described in this text, is extremely powerful and sensitive. It cannot be properly performed by an incumbent who is "one of the boys." Should he ease into one or more cliques, association with these factions may be gained at the apparent expense of his impartiality and neutrality. If a clique forms around him, it may cause his already threatening political posture to appear even more magnified. On the other hand, if he restricts himself only to professional interactions on official business, personal isolation is risked, and with it political emasculation.

Any one of these courses can increase anxiety and resentment toward company-wide planning within the organization. Perhaps a workable guide is for the chief planner to strive for professional respect, not personal popularity.

The planner must avoid being type-cast as to capacities and functions. Should he allow himself to be preoccupied with a particular level or sector of his own duties or with the organization at large, entree to others could be inhibited.

For instance, concentration on concept might earn him the title of "egg-head" which may close doors of those who fancy themselves "practical men" both within and outside of the organization. On the other hand, working largely on procedure could exclude him from the organizations's intellectual elite as a mere "plodder." Also, spending inordinate time in the area of technological research and development may taint him as its ally in the eyes of a rival function—say, Marketing. Unfortunately, in this matter, because "you're damned if you do and damned if you don't," only constant attention to balance in emphasis is an acceptable course.

For a chief planner, especially the initial incumbent, upstaging the chief executive can be very easy and even inadvertent. Establishment of a company-wide planning function usually portends significant changes in an organization. As the person directly responsible for conceptualization, installation, and operation of the company-wide planning system, the chief planner could be mistaken as the sole architect of grand innovation.

As purveyor of modern management technology to many in the organization, his reputation as an expert could snowball. As a key participant in what may be a new or revitalized program of liaison with the financial community, external observers could overestimate his impact and stature. And generally, as advisor and confidant of the chief executive, his pronouncements will be intensively recorded, analyzed, and disseminated as an indication of the future.

Thus the chief planner, especially the initial incumbent, may to some degree displace the chief executive as perceived thinker and spokesman for the organization. To the extent that this occurs, the planner may be taken as crown prince and heir apparent, with attendant political advantages and risks. His greatest worry, however, could well be the natural resentment of the chief executive. Therefore, to the chief planner, this identity may be a risky pastime engaged in only with full awareness of current and probable consequences.

While it may at first sound odd to the uninitiated, undue dedication can be unusually detrimental to the chief planner. Relentless pursuit of a formally approved program and schedule, especially when forced-drafted, can expose him to high political risks from all factions, within the organization and externally. The internal difficulties have already been sketched. Externally, he would be wise to safeguard and promote his reputation in professional and industry circles as a hedge for self-preservation.

By this time it must be obvious that the chief planner can easily find himself at the center of political upheaval. Should this occur, who would be concerned for him? Removal of the thorn is expedient whether right or wrong. Who would dare to help?

In summary, the role of chief planner is highly visible, extremely vulnerable, and conveniently expendable. In this position, disproportionate altruism and naïvete could lead to professional suicide.

# CHAPTER 18

# *Summary and Conclusions*

> *When wood is chopped, chips must fly.*
> —Polish proverb

## § 18.1 SOME FUNDAMENTALS REVIEWED

This book was concerned with planning, an activity defined throughout these pages as *a prescriptive process intended to guide discretionary decision-making in deployment and management of resources.*

The sphere of company-wide planning encompasses *all significant influences*, external and internal, effecting sustained surveillance for rationality, system, and consistency, of objectives, missions, policies, strategies, and estimates. The scope thus includes behavioral, technological, and financial parameters that meaningfully characterize the environment outside of and within the organization. This approach necessitates matching controls to detect anomalies in rationality, system, and consistency, within and between organization units and time periods.

The accelerating rate of change in the business environment, and the new emphasis upon growth and diversification, coupled with mounting sophistication in management technology, has enlarged decision-making requirements in every dimension. Governments worldwide have intensified applications of formal planning which in turn encourage and reward like activity within the private enterprise sector.

The essential purpose of company-wide planning is to increase the probability that organization objectives will be attained. Toward this end, plans for future resource deployment are continuously developed and appraised for their compatibility with organization objectives and constraints. The company-wide planning system

- requires *estimates* of future organization performance and resources, over relevant time periods,
- *matches* these estimates with organization objectives during relevant time periods, and thereby
- determines the *gap* between these objectives and estimates, as to both magnitude and timing, which then
- *precipitates* means for closing this gap, by redeployment of organization resources and/or adjustment of performance standards, modification of parameters, or change in objectives and constraints.

This system requires an organization structured for centralized substance and decentralized procedure. Each planning cycle is an iterative set of oscillations between top-down specifications for organization performance and bottom-up estimates of performance expected, in order to resolve discrepancies between the two. If the desired magnitude, complexity, and frequency of recycling become too onerous, or if a shorter reaction time is sought, the planning system must itself be significantly redesigned, administratively and technologically.

The uniqueness in this form of planning rests upon four major characteristics:

- a total environments viewpoint,
- application of scientific method,
- clear and precise objectives,
- integration of strategy and operations.

To the extent these do not dominate, the company-wide planning function has yet to be effectively internalized.

Some readers may still suspect that the entire scheme presented in this text is a giant circularity. This cannot be true because the organization is open to impacts of an external environment which is far from a controlled element in the system. Utility of company-wide planning as described herein will ultimately be reflected in the significance or triviality, success or failure, of actions and responses it precipitates and monitors.

## § 18.2  THE BENEFITS RECEIVED

The benefits of company-wide planning reflect values from the philosophy of science, modern management theory, and normal business practice:

- Detection of problems, major and minor, is made more probable sufficiently in advance to spur timely remedy.

- Rationality, system, and consistency are promoted and facilitated.
- Recall of values, facts, and reasoning is enabled through documentation.
- Political controversy may be mitigated through the resulting depersonalization and group pressure.
- Leadership may be augmented by system-precipitated requirements for decisions.
- Management development is enhanced for those professionals associated with this multifaceted activity.
- Greater compatibility of management systems and data forms with those of other businesses and government is made more likely.
- Financial community relations are aided through the broader scope, data compatibility, and confidence engendered.

In summary, company-wide planning is likely to make more effective the process of resource deployment and the management of those resources once deployed. In conclusion, it is *the process of planning, and not the plan itself,* which results in benefits cited.

## § 18.3 IS IT WORTH IT TO THE PLANNER?

For those who possess the personal characteristics specified in § 17.2, there is no better role than that of planner in which to obtain maximum opportunity for

- exercise of *intellectual scope*, relatively unfettered by administrative trivia
- opportunity to advance the frontiers of *manage-*

*ment technology*, both within the host organization and for the profession as a whole

- *exposure* to topmost management, inside the organization and externally
- unusually competent, broad, and stimulating superiors, peers, and subordinates, in a *professional* environment
- opportunity to *learn* the organization's functioning in all processes, products, markets, and locales
- *contribution* to the host organization per se, and to the industry(ies) of which it is a member

As pointed out in § 17.3, the psychological dimensions, vocational attributes, and behavioral characteristics of those truly qualified to be planners equip them better than most. However, because of his personal orientation, the planner prefers this profession to activities of a different sort which may be more beneficial financially.

For his privileges, the planner must pay in other ways as well. He will be condescendingly tagged "a technician" by those who superficially understand his role or perhaps are jealous of his capacities. His unusual dedication may be thought "odd" by many and "risky" by some. Those who are too lazy to meet him halfway and others promoting his demise may shake their heads in mock sorrow and say "if he could only communicate," or with greater deceit, "no one understands what he is talking about." And at the very least, he will probably be treated as a de facto inferior relative to the traditionally prestigeous operating personnel.

Because the planner starts at a high level in the organization he therefore can dead-end rapidly. Fortunately, the process of planning is universal, and so, the planner's concepts and techniques are readily transferable within and between organizations. On the other hand, should the planner be interested in and temperamentally fitted for pursuing operations responsibilities, no background could be better preparation than his. In fact, some may purposely commence their careers in the planning function as an early stepping-stone to top management.

Thus, while the planner is, by the nature of his work, a bobbing cork on an ocean of political instability, his personal capacities and functional flexibility permit healthy survival and rapid advancement provided he is willing to be mobile. If he perceives and executes his role as described in this book, and acts in the manner suggested above, the planning function offers among the highest and most volatile risks and rewards in all of management.

Whatever their other motivations and aspirations, those who are fortunate enough to possess the personal characteristics specified in § 17.2 have the social responsibility, technical competence, and professional discipline required to face and surmount the very severe challenges of the true planner.

Should such qualified personnel choose to be planners, they will reap the unusual satisfaction of this role to benefit us all. I strongly encourage them to do so.

## § 18.4  IS IT WORTH IT TO THE COMPANY?

As noted in § 1.5, the real costs of company-wide planning transcend those disclosed through conventional accounting. The intervening text has had a continually throbbing undertone supporting initial contentions that the most expensive elements directly attributable to company-wide planning per se are

- the great amounts of executive time devoted to planning-related matters,
- the technical and administrative support by staff and service units, and
- dissonance and strain necessarily surrounding the change precipitated by this function.

However, cost, tangible and intangible, explicit and implicit, to be fairly appraised, should be judged relative to benefits derived. The cost-benefit relationship is adjustable on both sides of the equation. When applied to the company-wide planning function per se, intangibles and imponderables abound. In this type of decision-making, high reliance must be placed upon judgment.

Given the truly enormous importance of the company-wide planning function, only topmost management can be permitted to establish and maintain its cost-benefit balance. Miscalculation on this matter can be, at the very least, extremely expensive and very embarrassing. From this minimal base, unchecked misapplication could severely damage the organization and destroy careers of those associated with that function.

Thus, effective use of company-wide planning is, as with all other facets of management, a matter of appropriate degree and pattern. Its orientation, form, and sophistication should fit circumstances and intentions. Suitably guided and competently directed, company-wide planning, as described in this book, has promising potential for all concerned.

The process of planning is itself a manifestation of human creativity in that it seeks to better apply this scarce and powerful attribute in a rational, systematic, and consistent manner throughout the organization. Regretfully, while the planning function can extend and multiply human creativity, it can never substitute for it.

# INDEX